Living Sent
The Disciple Maker's Handbook

An individual and group guide for
Everyone Sent to Multiply Everything

Robin Wallar

Hamilton, Ontario, Canada

Contact Information:
info@liftchurch.ca
P.O. Box 89120
991 King St. W.
Hamilton, ON
L8S 4R5

Contents

Part 4 Radical Generosity

Part 5 Crucial Conversations

Living Sent

Acknowledgements

This was a collaborative work that would not be possible without the tireless work of many people. In particular, thank you to Dan Lupo and Nicole Haverkamp. Your insights, suggestions and contributions to the content, and especially the response questions, made this project possible. Mikaela Ferguson, Emma Lelea and Merna Moshi thank you for your creative input. Ellen Bedecki, thank you for your editorial work! There are many others whose efforts are not seen, but know that you are deeply appreciated!

Thank you to my wife, Laura for her patience, sacrifice and support to get this work completed! I am more grateful than you know!

Preface

This book was written as an accompanying guide to my first book, *Everyone Sent to Multiply Everything (ESME)*. There were two primary motivations behind the completion of this accompanying handbook. Firstly, the dominant feedback from the ESME book was that people needed more concrete applications and a simplifying of the ideas to make them more accessible to a broader audience. Secondly, while ESME outlined a robust framework for discipleship, it did not provide a specific guide to discipleship conversations. Consequently, practical discipleship was still mysterious and confusing to many people. This handbook seeks to help people feel more confident engaging in actual discipleship conversations by providing a structure and format for the dialogue.

Robin Wallar
Hamilton, Ontario
June 2020

Getting Started

How to Use This Book

This book is intended to be worked through in the context of discipleship relationships. It could work one-on-one or in a group setting. Each chapter, or session, has two parts: preparation and discipleship.

Preparation

Individually read one chapter at a time. Each chapter has four main parts: scripture, teaching, response questions and a section for questions you have for your discipler.

Be sure to read the scripture reading before proceeding into the body of the chapter, as the scripture passages lay an important foundation for the teaching.

Each chapter includes a teaching section with scripture and quotations woven throughout. The teaching sections are not intended to be a comprehensive account of each subject but rather a starting point for a healthy dialogue with your discipler.

With that in mind, as you work your way through the chapters, take time to respond on your own to the questions posed along the way. You are encouraged to make notes directly in the book to help you track your progress and stay focussed.

Take a moment at the end of each chapter to write down questions you have for your discipler. They may or may not have an answer, but this way you can explore possible answers together.

Many chapters include a Further Scripture Reading and Resources section that provides you with additional material on the content in each chapter. In many cases, you can find additional resources at: engage.liftchurch.ca under "Discipleship Resources."

Discipleship

After working through the preparation phase, you can gather in a small group or one-on-one with each of the disciples. These sessions will focus on a fairly simple, repeatable formula that can be used on any piece of scripture by asking four very simple questions:

1) What did this teach us about God?
2) What did this teach us about ourselves?
3) What steps of obedience could we take?
4) What next steps will we take?

In addition to these four questions, each discipleship session includes a time for celebration and praise, dialogue of questions, review of the previous session and, of course, prayer.

Tips for discipleship sessions:

1) Schedule them in advance and honour the schedule.

2) Set up a consistent rhythm of every week or every other week.

3) You may find that there is too much content in each chapter to cover in a single session. If that is the case, you are encouraged to split the sessions into two. It is better to prioritize depth and formation than merely seek to complete the content. Work through the content at a pace that is helpful for both disciple and discipler.

4) Remember the three ingredients and four steps. Do not limit the discipleship relationship to just these sessions.

5) Pray. Every time.

With these tools in hand, jump in and open your heart to Jesus' transformation through this discipleship journey!

Introduction:
Welcome, Disciple

Welcome to the journey of becoming a disciple-making disciple! Every follower of Jesus is a part of an unbroken chain of disciple-making disciples that traces their origin all the way back to Jesus himself in Matthew 28.

Matthew 28:19-20 [ESV]

Go therefore and make disciples of all nations, baptizing them in the name of the Father and of the Son and of the Holy Spirit, teaching them to observe all that I have commanded you. And behold, I am with you always, to the end of the age."

That unbroken chain of discipleship is made up of disciples who made other disciples, all the way down through the ages. Standing firm in Jesus' promise of his presence, disciples through time have committed themselves to knowing Jesus and inviting others to do the same. Today, as with disciples throughout history, each of us who have come to discover the glorious joy of a saving relationship with Jesus have been able to do so because of the work of a disciple in our lives. This is the work of someone who has embraced the invitation of Jesus to 'live sent.' Living sent is all about walking in a vibrant relationship with Jesus such that the world around us discovers him by witnessing him in our lives. In this book, we are inviting you to both be discipled and to disciple others and, in so-doing, serve as another link in the chain of discipleship. This beautiful calling to be a disciple-making disciple is no small thing; indeed, your soul will be strengthened such that you will know the depths of the love of the one who has made you. Likewise, you will discover that through his work in your life, he will accomplish more than you could ever ask or imagine. May you receive this prayer that the Apostle Paul prayed over his disciples thousands of years ago in Ephesians 3:

Ephesians 3:14-21

For this reason I kneel before the Father from whom every family in heaven and on earth is named. I pray that he may grant you, according to the riches of his glory, to be strengthened with power in your inner being through his Spirit, and that Christ may dwell in your hearts through faith. I pray that you, being rooted and firmly established in love, may be able to comprehend with all the saints what is the length and width, height and depth of God's love, and to know Christ's love that surpasses knowledge, so that you may be filled with all the fullness of God.

Now to him who is able to do above and beyond all that we ask or think according to the power that works in us—to him be glory in the church and in Christ Jesus to all generations, forever and ever. Amen.

As you commit to the journey of discipleship, you will be stretched, challenged and encouraged along the way. This process involves four simple repeating steps to follow, along with three crucial ingredients for you to invest into the process. For each of the sessions, you will need to put all of these into practice. As you embrace a discipleship relationship, it is absolutely essential that you commit to all four steps and all three ingredients, as a robust discipleship process will involve all of them working in unison together.

Three Ingredients to Invest

There are three essential ingredients that both the discipler and the disciple invest into the relationship: time, proximity and vulnerability. These are indispensable, and there is no short-cut around them. It is important that they are incorporated by both parties in a discipleship relationship. Perhaps the greatest challenge is that these ingredients are contrary to many of our natural tendencies or desires. Discipleship is often a slow, intentional and sacrificial journey. For this reason, Jesus invited his disciples to "count the cost" before they committed to following him (Luke 14:28-30).

Time Together

Discipleship requires that we invest into one another's lives over a period of time. This might sound obvious, but in a world where instant and immediate results are expected, it bears repeating. A discipleship relationship is not a casual acquaintance with whom you receive pearls of wisdom when the timing is suitable, nor is it reduced to occasional coffees. Discipleship is an intentional commitment to invest relationally in another person through thick and thin. This means that discipleship is not an action taken in response to a person's specific need at one point in time — a mentorship or counselling relationship would be more appropriate for that. Discipleship is not about fixing issues or dealing with the way you have fallen short or sinned most recently. In a discipleship relationship, we are continually pointing people to Jesus so that they can, in turn, do the same for others. In a discipleship relationship, our primary job is to see people living lives in light of the Gospel. As a result, it takes time to see this bear fruit. It requires patience to allow the process to work.

Proximity to Each Other

The second ingredient of discipleship is that it requires proximity. This means that we are "in each other's world." Discipleship requires that our lives are intertwined. Jesus' ministry was one of intentional engagement with the people around him. Those Jesus was discipling were intimately involved in each other's lives. They ate together, travelled together, worked together and even shared living quarters.

We like to use the phrase "up in each other's business." Discipleship is a means by which we are so involved in each other's lives that there is ample opportunity to observe both the positive and negative in the actions and words of one another. Proximity means that we cannot hide who we are; there are no masks or pretend Christians in these relationships.

It is worth noting that this kind of relationship is only possible by the grace of Jesus. The friction that can result in this type of situation requires that we demonstrate supernatural grace and love towards one another. Perhaps this is part of the reason why John writes so emphatically in 1 John to love one another as believers.

If the natural rhythm of our life is not amenable to effective discipleship, then we have no alternative but to change the rhythm of our lives to allow that to happen. Jesus has given us a command to make disciples; if the setup of our life is not helping that happen, then we need to change the setup of our life. This may mean changes in where we work, where we live, where and how we are engaged in a church family, or even how we spend our money. This simple ingredient of proximity is closely linked to missional living; we cannot live missionally without having proximity to the people Jesus has placed in our lives to disciple.

Vulnerability

The final ingredient is that of intentional vulnerability on both sides of discipleship relationship. Discipleship requires that our lives are open to one another. Again, from observing Jesus' ministry, he was profoundly vulnerable with his disciples. They saw him weep at the death of friends and show fear in the face of death. The Gospel writers go out of their way to highlight Jesus' humanity — exhaustion, weariness, fear and grief. The fact that they could write about this means that Jesus had been vulnerable enough to allow them to see him at his weakest!

Time and proximity do not automatically produce vulnerability. There are people with whom we spend a great deal of time and proximity but whom we may not really know; often, co-workers or fellow students would fall into this category. It is through vulnerability that our lives are opened up and the transformational work of Jesus is ultimately revealed to the person we are discipling. Vulnerability is about inviting a person into a relationship that is not merely transactional but is actually a relationship of intimacy. The fact that vulnerability is a key ingredient for growing in discipleship potential is liberating because it means that healthy discipleship relationships do not require us to be strong, perfect or to have all the answers all the time. In fact, it is in our weaknesses, fears, doubts and concerns that the person we are discipling can see who we really are and the degree to which Christ is moving in us.

Discipleship is a process where we open our lives for people to see how Christ moves in us and may also move in them. As our lives are opened, Christ moves through our lives to transform theirs. The supreme joy of discipleship is that it is not about us but is about what Jesus is doing. This means that our vulnerability, especially in our weaknesses, is a powerful tool in the hands of the Holy Spirit.

It is worth mentioning that if there is very close proximity and a high degree of vulnerability, then the amount of time required can certainly be shortened, as illustrated in Jesus' own ministry. In a mere three years, he was able to raise incredible leaders who, when empowered by the Spirit, would initiate the birth of the Church. This is why high-proximity situations, such as sharing a house or travelling together, and high-vulnerability situations, such as processing grief or confessing habitual sin, can be so powerful in moving a discipleship relationship forward.

Respond

Have you taken time to reflect on the sacrificial cost of discipleship as you enter into an intentional discipleship relationship?

Which ingredient (time, proximity or vulnerability) do you think you will find the most challenging and why?

Four Steps to Follow

How then does discipleship actually happen? How do we mix these three ingredients — what is the recipe, so to speak? How do we intentionally and proactively engage with people in a way that leads them to be made alive in Christ and subsequently to see others also made alive in Christ? How do we disciple people in a way that consistently and reliably results in a multiplication of disciples? There are four steps to follow to be an effective discipler.

Invite

Discipleship starts with an invitation to relationship. "Follow me" (Matthew 4:19a) were the first words that Jesus spoke to the disciples. This invitation went far deeper than merely an invitation to a relationship. It was an invitation to a life of mission: "and I will make you fish for people" (Matthew 4:19b). Discipleship is not the same as an invitation to friendship, though friendship will certainly result from it! Discipleship is an invitation for others to join us in experiencing life in Christ so that they can do the same with those in their world.

This crucial step of discipleship is often the easiest, but also the scariest. Oftentimes, extending or receiving an invitation means exposing ourselves to vulnerability. We may be rejected; we may feel under-equipped or afraid of failure; however, discipleship is ultimately the work of the Holy Spirit. While we are inviting people to come be with us, we are ultimately inviting them not to ourselves but to join in what Christ is doing through us. When we extend or receive an invitation, we do so with a profound reliance on the Holy Spirit to work in that person, such that, through us, Christ will be formed in them. The starting point of this is laying the groundwork in prayer. "Lord, who can I invite to know you or be in a relationship with you?"

It is also worth mentioning that this invitation is applied to all areas. Extending invitations is not restricted to non-believers. We are constantly inviting people to come be with us. Every day, the prayer is "who can I invite to be with me in this mission that Jesus has called me to?" That may mean inviting someone to take a step towards increased leadership responsibility; it may mean inviting them to stretch themselves in a way that they are not sure they are able or it may be an invitation to take a leap of faith. It is through invitations that we both initiate and maintain momentum in the discipleship process.

Model

Secondly, discipleship is an invitation for people to come and observe our lives and copy them, and for you to observe and imitate your discipler. It is in this step that the tremendous potential impact of discipleship lies. In 1 Corinthians 10:31-11:1, Paul invites the churches to imitate him in matters as simple as eating and drinking and illustrates how everything he does reflects and points people to Jesus.

1 Corinthians 10:31-11:1

So, whether you eat or drink, or whatever you do, do everything for the glory of God. Give no offence to Jews or Greeks or the church of God, just as I also try to please everyone in everything, not seeking my own benefit, but the benefit of many, so that they may be saved. Imitate me as I imitate Christ.

Similarly, when Jesus called the disciples to follow him, it was an invitation to an intentional and transparent community. There is no divide between the sacred and the secular in this aspect of discipleship. We are inviting people to examine every dimension of our lives so that they can observe a desire, willingness and obedience to see Jesus as Lord.

The temptation in discipleship is to restrict our modelling of Christ to formal "discipleship moments," to invite people to model after us in only the restricted areas to which we give them access. The true power of discipleship lies in vulnerably opening our lives up so that people can see how Jesus is living in us. As a result of this step in discipleship, the question that must be continually asked is: "is this aspect of my life reflecting Jesus, and do I want those I am discipling to copy it?"

If we are not careful, the invitation to discipleship can result in us replicating the patterns of the world instead of the Kingdom of Jesus. We are constantly being "discipled" by the world around us and have to be careful to identify the ways in which our lives are modelled after the prevalent decision making processes of our culture, typically called social norms. For example, we often unintentionally model through our lives and decisions that career is more important than the Kingdom. The subtle ways our lives are modelled after worldly culture instead of Kingdom culture requires that we are continually returning to scripture with humility to allow the way we are living to be turned upside down.

Train

The third step is training: the intentional learning and transmission of practices, knowledge, attitudes and techniques for producing followers of Jesus through our discipleship efforts. Training is the step where we pass along the important tools and information to help people thrive in their journey with Jesus and to be able to pass along wisdom and understanding to others.

In the process of producing multiplying disciples of Jesus, it is important that they are equipped with a high-quality, transmittable and doctrinally sound understanding of the Gospel. While the Gospel is profoundly simple in one sense, it is also tremendously deep. A lifetime of study would not unearth all the riches that it contains. Formulating a solid foundation of gospel fluency in each person we disciple is critical for them to produce disciples themselves.

There are three fatal errors that we can make when considering this step of discipleship. First, we run the risk of thinking that training is merely the transmission of information. Information is important of course, but it is only a starting point. Part of training is to see that information moves from 'head' to 'heart' in the people we are discipling. This is accomplished through vulnerability.

There is a tremendous cost to following Jesus. Jesus himself reminds us in Matthew 16:24 that the cost of following him is, in fact, an invitation to adopt an execution device. "When Christ calls a man he bids him, come and die" as the famous theologian, Dietrich Bonhoeffer, famously said in his work *The Cost of Discipleship*. We are training people in the way of dying to themselves and living instead with the ambition of making the Gospel known (2 Corinthians 5:20). This clearly extends far beyond information transmission; rather, it is training people for a life of discipleship. We must resist the desire for discipleship to be an easy or comfortable process for both the discipler and the one being discipled. We must confront, with grace and love but also truth, those we are discipling.

Participating in a training course, working through a curriculum or listening to a podcast may be helpful in providing fuel for discussion and activation for the disciple, however they do not serve as the basis of discipleship. The basis of our discipleship must be an invitation to share time, proximity and vulnerability with us and, in so doing, open our lives so that as Christ is formed in us, he will also be formed in those we are discipling.

The second potential pitfall in the training process is when we restrict discipleship to training without connecting it to the other essential steps of invitation, modelling and empowering. As we have articulated above, we cannot properly disciple people without engaging the whole of the person with the whole of ourselves. This can only be done when we vulnerably open up our lives to them to see Christ formed in us. Discipleship is not, strictly speaking, a student-teacher relationship. In a traditional mentality, the teacher does not and should not open the whole of their life to their student for them to examine and replicate it.

Our training in discipleship must include an active practice of invitation and a sharing of time, proximity and vulnerability with those we are discipling.

Third, we can run the risk of over-complicating the discipleship process; instead, we should focus on the basics. The concepts are straightforward to understand and, as a result, easy to transmit. Focussing the bulk of our energy on the basics of the Gospel allows us to truly be formed by scripture and see ourselves empowered to do the same with others.

Empower

The final step in discipleship is the act of empowering the person we are discipling to begin to disciple people themselves. The importance of this step in discipleship cannot be overstated. This is the step where the disciple is 'living sent.'

Jesus did not teach and train his disciples to merely comprehend or even be transformed by his teaching. Very early in the discipleship journey, he empowered the disciples to carry out the same work that he was doing.

Luke 9:1-2

Summoning the Twelve, he gave them power and authority over all the demons and to heal diseases. Then he sent them to proclaim the kingdom of God and to heal the sick.

He gave them real power and real authority to go on a real mission to genuinely proclaim the Kingdom to those who may not listen. Jesus' empowerment of the disciples was not a carefully sanitized micro-version of ministry in which there was no risk. He sent them to those who could just as easily reject them. Early in the discipleship journey, Jesus empowers his disciples to do what he did. In fact, after just three years, he entrusted the entire mission to them! As Alan Hirsch says of Jesus' empowerment, "talk about a baptism of fire."

In empowering the disciples, Jesus exposed them early on to three very important principles of discipleship. First, he demonstrated that they had a responsibility to the mission that went far deeper than merely following Jesus or doing what he said. They needed to become active contributors to the mission. There is no room in the Kingdom of God for mere consumption. Every one of us is called to ministry and, as a result, must take on ownership of the mission of God.

As a second principle of discipleship, Jesus exposed them to the reality of failure. Discipleship is not a straightforward linear process in which the only direction we go is up. It is filled with ups and downs; there will always be both success and failures.

When he sends the disciples, Jesus tells them to expect failure as a part of the process (Luke 10:10). By empowering disciples to go and make other disciples early in the process, we can create a more failure-tolerant culture, in which people are more willing to put themselves out there at the risk of failure. The problem is not the failure itself but rather how they respond to the failure. In empowering early in the process, the disciples are exposed to failure early and as a result become more resilient to it.

Third, Jesus exposed them to the joy of success on the mission. In the Gospel of Luke, Jesus sends out 72 disciples to proclaim the news about Jesus. When they return, they boldly proclaim that even the demons submitted to Jesus name! They quickly get a "win" under their belts which has the tremendous effect of emboldening them in their willingness to make disciples. Seeing someone respond to discipleship, whether it is a total life transformation in becoming a believer or grasping a small truth, is tremendously encouraging for the discipler. By empowering the disciples early in the discipleship journey, Jesus was inviting them to discover the joy of partnering with the mission of God. It is in this partnership that we invite our disciples to discover a whole new kind of joy! The greatest tragedy would be if we withheld from them the joy of seeing God move through them to transform someone else's heart.

Experiential learning is perhaps one of the greatest ways that we grow as disciples. The requirement to begin teaching, communicating and sharing our faith will actually result in refining our ability to do so. In discipleship, practice indeed does make perfect — or at least helps us grow closer to the perfect discipleship that Jesus modelled for us.

Summary

When the four steps of discipleship work together, each disciple should become a disciple-making disciple. Jesus initiated the process of inviting, modelling, training and empowering with his disciples, and we walk in the rich history of millions of disciple-making disciples down through the ages. The inviting, training, modelling and empowering of disciples is not a one-time set of actions but a continual cycle with the people we are discipling. As we empower them, we also continue to invite them into relationship, and to continue to grow in their discipleship capacity. In this way, those we are discipling are simultaneously activated for multiplication and continued personal formation.

Respond

Which of the four steps are you most excited to experience yourself? Which one least?

Have you invited someone to disciple you? Have you invited someone to be discipled by you?

Summary

Welcome to *Living Sent*. It is our prayer that as you study scripture, spend time in prayer and walk in an intentional discipleship relationship, you discover the supreme joy of participating in a discipleship movement. We pray that the Holy Spirit speaks loudly and clearly to you, that you obey his voice and that you walk with boldness and confidence into the calling of disciple-making. As the Apostle Paul prayed, *"Now to him who is able to do above and beyond all that we ask or think according to the power that works in us— to him be glory in the church and in Christ Jesus to all generations, forever and ever. Amen."*

So, let's begin.

1
What is Discipleship?

Welcome to your first discipleship session! In this session, we are going to tackle the question, "What is discipleship?" As you begin or continue your journey of discipleship, it is important to understand Jesus' heart for disciple-making. Take a moment and reflect on what it means for you to be a disciple. Pray by yourself as you read these scriptures.

Scripture Reading

To help you prepare, read the following scriptures on your own:

- [ ] Matthew 28:16-20
- [ ] 2 Thessalonians 1:11-12
- [ ] Romans 6:22
- [ ] John 15:8
- [ ] James 2:26

Respond

From the above scriptures, write your own definition of discipleship. What does it mean to be a follower of Jesus?

Discipleship As Worship

Matthew 28:19-20

Go, therefore, and make disciples of all nations, baptizing them in the name of the Father and of the Son and of the Holy Spirit,

*teaching them to observe everything I have commanded you.
And remember, I am with you always, to the end of the age.*

The Great Commission to make disciple-making disciples, as found in Matthew 28:16-20, is among one of the most well-known and often-cited verses from scripture. However, what exactly is disciple-making all about?

Fundamentally, discipleship is about God getting the glory that he deserves. Discipleship is about worship. Until we correctly understand the principle that discipleship is ultimately about God's glorification, we will struggle to be effective in seeing ourselves walk as multiplying disciples.

The fact that discipleship, and indeed all Christian life, is about worship is central to a proper and robust understanding of the Gospel. As we will discuss in detail later, we receive new life, freedom and purpose by receiving the grace of Jesus. We are invited to receive life and life to the full by participation in the life of Jesus (John 10:10). While it is true that we receive a tremendous gift by accepting the life Jesus has, it can cause us to think that discipleship is about us. Emphatically stated, discipleship is a means by which we glorify God. Discipleship IS worship.

To fully understand the fact that discipleship is worship, we must examine Jesus' own life and the ultimate purpose of his mission. At a basic level, discipleship is following Jesus; therefore, Jesus' purpose must become our purpose.

John 17:1

Father, the hour has come. Glorify your Son so that the Son may glorify you

Jesus came and died so that God would be glorified! The entire Gospel narrative is ultimately about restoring God to his place of worship in humanity. The Gospel is not about us; discipleship is not about us; the church is not about us; it is all about him!

We may be tempted to be offended by this concept as we may pridefully think, "Who does God think he is to desire worship?" The answer is that he is God! He is all-powerful, all-knowing, entirely-good, creator-God of the universe! God has the right and the authority to demand worship. Instead of doing so, he has invited us to worship as a free choice in response to his self-sacrificial love.

The principle of discipleship as worship is essential because it forms the basis of our heart for discipleship by shifting our attention off of ourselves and onto the Father. It is also a practical building block since the journey of discipleship will undoubtedly be uncomfortable, painful and difficult, as Jesus himself has promised (Luke 14:26-28). The call to discipleship is ultimately a call to die to ourselves and to live a life of worship.

Luke 14:27

Whoever does not bear his own cross and come after me cannot be my disciple.

When Christ calls a man he bids him, come and die.[1]
— Dietrich Bonhoeffer

Many of the disciples, and the second generation disciples, suffered and even died for their faith (1 Peter 1:6, Acts 7:60). How were they able to do this? Because they knew it was not about them. If we think that discipleship, and by extension multiplication and the church as a whole, is about us, we will never be able to walk the road of discipleship that Jesus has called us to; it is simply too costly. Discipleship is an invitation to properly position our lives at the throne of God in surrender and declare, "*My life is no longer mine — use it for your glory.*"

1 Peter 4:11

If anyone speaks, let it be as one who speaks God's words; if anyone serves, let it be from the strength God provides, so that God may be glorified through Jesus Christ in everything. To him be the glory and the power forever and ever. Amen.

All of this talk of glorification has an unbelievable, even shocking, implication: through discipleship, we not only get to give glory to God, a supreme privilege in itself, we are also glorified in the process ourselves!

Romans 8:17

We suffer with him so that we may also be glorified with him.

Think about that for a moment: by living lives of sacrificial discipleship, we get to give glory and also be recipients of it! The supreme grace of God is that we get to receive his glory! He gives glory to us so that we can return the glory to him.

Respond

Have you thought about discipleship as a kind of self-help? How does the vision that discipleship is all about worship change what you hope to accomplish in making disciples?

Have you considered that evangelism (multiplication) and discipleship are an act of worship? How does this truth change the way you view discipleship and multiplication?

What is Discipleship?

How is God glorified in our discipleship? Discipleship is to follow and be transformed by Jesus. However, for many of us, that is where it stops in our thinking. We tend to think of discipleship as an individual, private pursuit. In reality, this could not be further from the truth. Discipleship is a relational process whereby we are invited to follow Jesus and are doing the same with others. It results in a total transformation in every aspect of our lives: relationships, family, career, finance, identity and, of course, worldview. Discipleship transformation inevitably results in this radical change multiplied into other people. Such a transformation is internal and external to who we are. We call these the inner-life and outer-life components of discipleship. As illustrated below:

A Holistic Picture of Discipleship

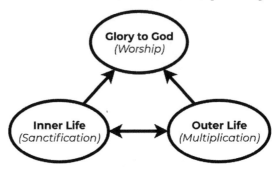

By combining the three components of discipleship — worship, sanctification and multiplication — we have the following definition of discipleship:

Glorifying God by following and being transformed by Jesus while inviting, modelling, training and empowering others to do likewise.

2 Thessalonians 1:11-12 paints a picture of discipleship as living a life worthy of his calling and producing good work through faith so that Jesus will be glorified.

2 Thessalonians 1:11-12

In view of this, we always pray for you that our God will make you worthy of his calling, and by his power fulfill your every desire to do good and your work produced by faith, so that the name of our Lord Jesus will be glorified by you, and you by him, according to the grace of our God and the Lord Jesus Christ.

Inner-Life — Sanctification

By 'inner-life,' we are referring to the process of becoming more like Jesus in our thoughts, words and actions. We recognize that everyone has parts of their lives that need transformation. There needs to be a continual process of identifying and repenting from sin. In its place, we learn to value and pursue the things of Jesus. We do not just focus on what we see externally, but we seek to see people experience a total heart transformation (Ezekiel 36:26). The process of personal transformation is what we broadly call 'sanctification' in theological terms.

Romans 6:22 [ESV]

But now that you have been set free from sin and have become slaves of God, the fruit you get leads to sanctification and its end, eternal life.

As disciples, we are transformed to live as people no longer enslaved to sin, but walking as people whose purpose is to glorify God. The sanctification process is a means by which we are slowly moulded more and more into the person of Jesus.

Inner-life transformation is a deep uprooting of our soul. The process is often challenging, even painful, as we are matured into the likeness of Jesus (James 1:4). Inner-life transformation requires that we both know what Jesus is like and begin to look more like him in our lives.

One important aspect of inner-life transformation is learning to walk in security and harmony with the Spirit of God. Jesus invites us in John 15 to abide in him, meaning to find our security and hope in him. Inner-life discipleship, although challenging, is supremely life-giving, in part because we learn that our security, confidence and identity is in him. When we are grounded and abiding in Jesus, we can withstand any challenge or obstacle and need not have any fear. As we learn to have a secure inner life, we can live tremendously sacrificially without fear of burn-out, exhaustion, poverty or weakness, because Jesus sustains us. A secure inner life is the most stable, secure and peaceful life imaginable, even in an insecure, unstable and chaotic environment! The Apostle Paul emphatically makes the statement from prison in Philippians 4:12 that regardless of the situation, he has learned to be content. Similarly, David writes in Psalm 27:1 that the Lord is his light and his salvation and, as a result, he lives without fear.

Respond

What specific aspects of your life have you already seen Jesus "sanctify" (make like him)? In which parts do you know that he still has work to do? Share your thoughts with your discipler.

In what ways are you practically "abiding" in Jesus? Take a moment to sit in silence. What are thankful for?

Outer-Life — Multiplication

The second dimension is what we refer to as 'outer-life.' It is the work that is referred to in 2 Thessalonians 1 or the fruit referred to in John 15:8. Fruit in discipleship is our own disciples!

John 15:8

My Father is glorified by this: that you produce much fruit and prove to be my disciples.

By the 'outer-life' of discipleship, we are referring to the command to every believer to be a disciple-making disciple. Just as inner-life is the part of discipleship where sanctification happens; outer-life is the part of discipleship where multiplication occurs. Discipleship multiplication is an integral part of discipleship. It is not a component reserved for the elite but a requirement for everyone. The emphasis on multiplication in discipleship is an invitation to worship! Evangelism is an act of worship. When we properly understand this, we will no longer resist evangelism as an unfortunate Christian duty. Instead, evangelism becomes the natural, joyful result of us desiring to live lives of worship.

The calling to multiply disciples must not be restricted to the leadership of the church but must involve everyone! Every person in the church must understand their role as simultaneously being discipled and being a disciple-maker in their own right. Growing in discipleship is equal parts internal transformation (inner-life), and sharing and teaching others to do likewise (outer-life).

Outer-life is not the second step of discipleship; it is an indivisible and integral component of it. There is no inner-life transformation without outer-life multiplication. Scripture states it clearly that without multiplication in our discipleship, our faith is dead.

James 2:26

For just as the body without the spirit is dead, so also faith without works is dead.

Disciples multiply to other disciples. Disciples who do not multiply are not disciples. As Jesus himself states, we prove we are disciples by bearing fruit (John 15:8). It may sound harsh, but it is simply the teaching and invitation of Jesus.

Respond

What excites you about the truth/knowledge that you are a disciple-maker yourself? What are you hesitant about?

Is there someone you are discipling with whom you can share what you are learning? If not, is there someone you could talk to about beginning a discipleship relationship?

Discipleship Emphases

What are the aspects of following and being transformed by Jesus that we desire to see multiplied into others? We have come up with five areas to focus on, to help clearly answer the question: "What is it that we want to see multiplied in other people?" We call these the 5 Discipleship Emphases, which are:

Gospel Fluency

Our relationship to, understanding of and transformation by the Gospel, and our ability to multiply it into others.

Secure Identity

The reception of Jesus as Lord and the formation in us as children, servants and ambassadors of God.

Missional Living

An integrated life of surrender to Jesus, where we live to maximize our impact for the Kingdom of Jesus.

Radical Generosity

The giving of our time, talents and treasures in light of the radical generosity of God, who gave his Son first.

Crucial Conversations

The ability to enter into intentional, and often difficult, discipleship conversations about what Jesus is doing in our life or another's.

Respond

Which of the discipleship areas are you most confident in? Which one are you least confident in? Ask your discipler for their perspective on your strengths and weaknesses.

Summary

As you begin your journey towards being a multiplying disciple, we have laid out a few important aspects.

- The goal of discipleship is that we worship God.
- Discipleship is equal parts inner-life transformation outer-life multiplication.
- Inner-life transformation is a process called 'sanctification' and is where we begin to think and act like Jesus.
- Outer-life multiplication is where we disciple others.

Further Scripture Reading

To dive deeper into scripture on what talked about in this session, read:

- ☐ John 10:10
- ☐ Isaiah 49
- ☐ John 17:1
- ☐ Luke 14:26-28
- ☐ 1 Peter 4:11
- ☐ Romans 8:17
- ☐ Colossians 1:27-28

Questions for My Discipler

Write down a few questions that you would like to talk about with your discipler.

Discipleship Session 1

☐ Prayer

Spend time together in prayer, invite the Holy Spirit to guide your conversation. Take a moment to sit in silence as you prepare to listen to God's leading.

☐ Celebration

What can you celebrate since you last met? How is God moving in your lives? What discipleship stories can you share?

☐ Review Previous Session

Take a moment to review the previous session. Are there any discussion points or items that you need to follow up on?

☐ Scripture

Read two passages of scripture from the ones used in the session. Choose one that encouraged and one that challenged you.

☐ God

What are the primary attributes that you learned about God's character in this section? What encouraged or challenged you?

☐ Yourself

What did you learn about yourself from the above passages?

☐ Obedience

Does what you learned change the way you think?

Does what you learned about change the way you act?

Does what you learned about change the way you treat others?

☐ Questions

Take a moment to talk through the questions you had.

☐ Next Step

What is one step you can take between now and your next session to practice what you learned?

Who can you share what you learned with to help them know Jesus?

☐ Pray

Share concerns. Pray for one another. Invite the Holy Spirit to help you.

☐ Next Discipleship Session _____

Part 1

Gospel Fluency

2
God & Creation

Welcome to the second discipleship session! In this session we will give an introduction to gospel fluency and the first two gospel fluency moorings: God and creation. It is exciting that we get to start learning about gospel fluency by talking about God and his creation — which includes you! Ask the Holy Spirit to help you understand these concepts as you start.

Scripture Reading

To help you prepare, read the following scriptures on your own:

- ☐ Colossians 1:9-10
- ☐ Ephesians 2:4-5
- ☐ Genesis 1:1, 26-28
- ☐ Matthew 28:19
- ☐ Romans 1:19-20

Respond

What stands out to you about God's character from the above passages?

Gospel Fluency

The beginning of your discipleship journey starts with gospel fluency, the foundation of discipleship. It is the basic building block that all of the other discipleship emphases are built upon. Gospel Fluency is the area of discipleship that captures our awareness and comprehension of what Jesus has done and our ability to communicate that hope to others. At the most basic level, gospel fluency starts with the foundational truths of what Jesus has accomplished as revealed in scripture.

However, gospel fluency is more than mere intellectual assent to the narrative of the scriptures. Gospel fluency refers to a total life transformation in light of the Good News of Jesus. To be fluent in the Gospel is to have our entire worldview re-shaped in light of the Gospel. Such a complete transformation would, of course, include a reasonable understanding of theology and scripture but must extend to include a life lived in light of those truths.

Gospel fluency is about surrendering control of our lives in light of the incredible Good News of Jesus. It is an invitation to a radical life of total transformation, sanctification and mission! In order for us to accept the invitation to this radical life, the Holy Spirit must be working in our lives in two critical ways.

Colossians 1:9-10

We are asking that you may be filled with the knowledge of his will in all wisdom and spiritual understanding, so that you may walk worthy of the Lord, fully pleasing to him: bearing fruit in every good work and growing in the knowledge of God.

First, as Colossians 1:9-10 illustrates, gaining knowledge and understanding of the Gospel is a process that is made possible by the Holy Spirit. Second, the Holy Spirit will work to help develop the Godly knowledge and wisdom that we can use in our day to day lives. The Holy Spirit works to develop gospel fluency in both our inner life ("knowledge") and outer life ("good work"). This is God's incredible grace: that he would send the Holy Spirit to help us understand who he is and what he has done and then empower us to live in light of that knowledge!

Respond

From Colossians 1:9-10, why should we pursue gospel fluency?

Have you invited the Holy Spirit to help you understand the Gospel? Ask your discipler to pray with you, and invite the Holy Spirit to help you grow in this understanding.

What is the Gospel?

What is the Gospel? The Gospel is the good news that because of the death and resurrection of Jesus, you and I can have a relationship with God and be invited to a life of purpose. Everything centres on this work of Jesus. This miraculous event should change and inform the way we see our world, including our relationships, every aspect of our lives, all of creation and especially who God is.

Through Jesus' death and resurrection, we are invited to a new life with him. We are dead without Jesus, but by his grace, we are made fully alive. To be fully alive is to have a relationship with God and to invite others to as well. The good news of Jesus is not simply our debts being paid, but that we are invited to a new life of mission; a life dedicated to inviting others to be raised from death to life by the work of Jesus!

Ephesians 2:4-5 [ESV]

But God, being rich in mercy, because of the great love with which he loved us, even when we were dead in our trespasses, made us alive together with Christ—by grace, you have been saved

We, by our own effort, cannot raise ourselves to life. We are utterly lost without Jesus. However, in Jesus, we are raised from death to life. Not just life, but life to the fullest! The Gospel is both that we are made fully alive and that we are also called to invite others to be made fully alive!

The Gospel is news about how the Father sent the Son into the world so that we could be reconciled to him, and how, in turn, the Son sent the Holy Spirit so that we can be people of mission. To be fully alive is to live a life in harmony with the creator of the universe and to live a life marked by fruitfulness — to be disciple-making disciples. The former is the work of Jesus on this earth, and the latter is the work of the Holy Spirit in our lives. The Good News is incomplete without the empowerment of the Holy Spirit engaging us on mission!

In this missional view of the Gospel, the focus is on others. We cannot receive the Gospel without also receiving the call of the Gospel to see others invited to it — they are inseparable!

There are many important components to gospel fluency, but we must continually return to this basic building block: that we were dead in our sin, but by the grace of Jesus, we are invited to a new life of mission and joy.

> *But the Gospel transforms us so our self-understanding is no longer based on our performance in life. We are so evil and sinful and flawed that Jesus had to die for us. We were so lost that nothing less than the death of the divine Son of God could save us. But we are so loved and valued that he was willing to die for us. The Lord of the universe loved us enough to do that. So the Gospel humbles us into the dust and at the very same time exalts us to the heavens. We are sinners but completely loved and accepted in Christ at the same time.[2]*
> — Tim Keller

Respond

What does it mean that we are 'dead' in our sin?

Do you ever try to "earn" or "win" God's approval with your behaviour? Do you know that God already loves you? Do you believe that God already loves you?

Gospel Fluency Moorings

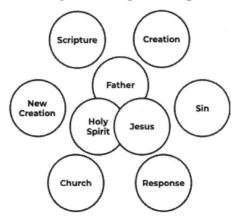

Do you believe that God wants to use you to bring the hope of Jesus to this world? Do you believe that God wants to use the people you are discipling to bring the hope of Jesus to this world? Do they know that you believe this? Do they believe it about themselves?

Gospel Fluency Moorings

There are so many ideas, concepts and perspectives that we hear each day, and we can easily become confused regarding what is true. To ensure that we are not blown about by these winds and waves of life (Ephesians 4:14), we must establish some core beliefs that can act as a foundation or mooring. Just as a mooring keeps a boat from drifting off to sea, strong theological moorings will help us not be led astray.

Ephesians 4:14

Then we will no longer be little children, tossed by the waves and blown around by every wind of teaching

To help provide clarity, we have developed 9 gospel fluency moorings that will help us grow as disciple-making disciples without going off track or getting distracted. Through the power of the Holy Spirit and in the context of the church community, these moorings will help us live our lives on mission in the world without becoming confused about what we believe.

These moorings are designed to encapsulate the grand narrative of scripture. For a concise, one-paged, narrative version of the moorings, see *Appendix A: The Story of Scripture.*

Respond

What ideas from our culture blow you around? How could you instead find stability in the Gospel?

God

We believe in God, who is love and is the creator and sustainer of all things. He exists in perfect harmony as three persons in one (we call it the Trinity). The Father, Son and Holy Spirit: a perfect, loving and glorious relationship. There is one God, who is sovereign over all creation, and all things exist for his glory. He is all-knowing, all-powerful and all-deserving of praise (Genesis 1:1, 2 Corinthians 13:13-14, Isaiah 43:7).

God is not like anything else — all metaphors or descriptions fail to entirely capture the magnitude of his glory. This is important because it means that we must humbly acknowledge that although God has revealed himself to us, we will never be able to fully comprehend the fullness of his glory.

There are two important applications of this mooring in the context of discipleship. First, we must continually point people to the supremacy of God over all. We are invited to humble ourselves before him and worship him because he is worthy of all praise. We worship him because of who he is! As Proverbs 9:10 says, "The fear of the Lord is the beginning of wisdom." Everything begins by acknowledging who God is.

The second aspect of this mooring is that it reminds us that God is relational in nature — the Trinity is a perfectly harmonious relationship. The relationship between Father, Son and Holy Spirit has been described by C.S. Lewis as an intimate dance involving each member of the Trinity — what a beautiful relational picture. The fact that God is relational is important because it means that he desires a relationship with his creation; although he is sovereign and supreme, he is knowable and wants you to know him! Expressed as love, God's nature is one of invitation to participate in his joy. God's sovereignty is not a cause for separation from him: our sin is. His sovereignty is the basis for security in a relationship with him since he is unchanging in his love for us (Exodus 3:14).

Respond

Which idea is easier for you to understand: God's supremacy or God's love?

Do you believe God desires a relationship with YOU?

What kinds of thoughts, actions or beliefs are preventing you from recognizing the supremacy of God?

And that, by the way, is perhaps the most important difference between Christianity and all other religions: that in Christianity God is not a static thing—not even a person—but a dynamic, pulsating activity, a life, almost a kind of drama. Almost, if you will not think me irreverent, a kind of dance. The union between the Father and Son is such a live concrete thing that this union itself is also a Person.[3]
— **C.S. Lewis**

Creation

Out of God's relational nature flows his creativity. The world around us was created by God, which means that it has a beginning. Distinct among his creation, God made you and I: humanity. We were created for relationship with God: to love and know him, each other and ourselves. In our pursuit of this, we were meant to be creative and adventurous. We were created in the image of God as his ambassadors on this earth. Therefore, we are meant to reflect his very nature. God's nature is creative, so our nature is to be creative. God's nature is relational, so our nature is relational.

In creating humanity, God has invited us into relationship and partnership with him. We were made to join the purposes of God from the very beginning of time. When we speak of multiplication, it is an invitation to re-engage our created purpose (Genesis 1:26-28, Matthew 28:19)!

Creation is good and valuable. The world around us does not always view creation this way. Humanity has dignity and value. How many people do not know that? How many people do not know that they have intrinsic and glorious worth? This is a beautiful truth that we need to proclaim! We must, as Romans 1:19-20 states, look to creation to understand God's nature and purposes.

Romans 1:20

For [God's] invisible attributes, that is, his eternal power and divine nature, have been clearly seen since the creation of the world, being understood through what he has made.

Living fully alive in Christ is to see alignment and harmony between the physical, emotional and spiritual aspects of who we are. As such, the value of creation applies to diverse areas such as sexuality, work, stewardship of the world and protecting the vulnerable. Part of raising disciples is inviting them to honour the created order. God has declared that creation is good, and we are both a part of that good creation and tasked with caring for it.

Respond

Do you believe that all people are valuable, precious and worthy of love? How does this belief change the way you treat people who are not close to you?

What are the subtle ways that you might not live that way?

How could you better care for creation?

Summary

In this session we gave an introduction to the Gospel as well as the first two of the nine moorings that help us be secure in our faith. We discovered that:

- Although there was nothing we could do so save ourselves, God redeemed us.
- We are dead in our sin, but fully alive in Jesus.
- God wants to use us to bring the hope of Jesus to the world around us.
- God is both sovereign and in-control.
- God is knowable and desires a relationship with us.
- We do not have to earn God's love; he gives it freely.
- Creation, especially humanity, has intrinsic worth and value.

Further Scripture Reading

If you would like to read more scripture on the topics in this session, please read:

☐ 2 Corinthians 13:13-14
☐ Isaiah 43:7
☐ Exodus 3:14

Questions For My Discipler

Write down a few questions that you would like to talk about with your discipler.

Discipleship Session 2

☐ Prayer

Spend time together in prayer, invite the Holy Spirit to guide your conversation. Take a moment to sit in silence as you prepare to listen to God's leading.

☐ Celebration

What can you celebrate since you last met? How is God moving in your lives? What discipleship stories can you share?

☐ Review Previous Session

Take a moment to review the previous session. Are there any discussion points or items that you need to follow up on?

☐ Scripture

Read two passages of scripture from the ones used in the session. Choose one that encouraged and one that challenged you.

☐ God

What are the primary attributes that you learned about God's character in this section? What encouraged or challenged you?

☐ Yourself

What did you learn about yourself from the above passages?

☐ Obedience

Does what you learned change the way you think?

Does what you learned about change the way you act?

Does what you learned about change the way you treat others?

☐ Questions

Take a moment to talk through the questions you had.

☐ Next Step

What is one step you can take between now and your next session to practice what you learned?

Who can you share what you learned with to help them know Jesus?

☐ Pray

Share concerns. Pray for one another. Invite the Holy Spirit to help you.

☐ Next Discipleship Session _____

3
Sin & Jesus

In this session, we will look at the next two gospel fluency moorings of sin and Jesus. These are two huge and challenging subjects, but they are so important to developing the ability to lead others to know Jesus. Take a moment and pray for understanding and wisdom as you begin.

Scripture Reading

To help you prepare, read the following scriptures on your own:

- [ ] Romans 6:23
- [ ] Romans 5:10
- [ ] Leviticus 20:26
- [ ] John 3:16-21
- [ ] John 1:1-14
- [ ] Matthew 5:1-11
- [ ] Acts 2:32-36

Respond

What stands out to you about God's view of sin? What stands out to you about Jesus' teaching and life?

Sin

While we were created for relationship with God, we so often choose to follow our own paths that lead us away from the plan God has for us. In doing so, we have ultimately rejected relationship with God. By trusting our own wisdom more than God's, we have opted to establish ourselves as gods in our own right. Our selfishness and pride have resulted in death entering our world. In choosing to reject a relationship with the author of life and creation, we also find ourselves separated from creation itself. As a result, we have a broken relationship with each other and the world around us. This rejection of a relationship with God is the root of what the scriptures call sin, and within ourselves, there is no solution.

The sinfulness of humanity can be a challenging truth to wrestle with. We have to acknowledge the bad news in order to have full access to the Good News. We are enemies of God; we have offended his glory and cut ourselves off from him. It is difficult to overstate the depth of our sin or the effects of our rebellion against God. We are sinners in desperate need of a saviour. We are dead in our sin — utterly and completely hopeless apart from the grace of Jesus (Romans 6:23).

Romans 6:23

For the wages of sin is death, but the gift of God is eternal life in Christ Jesus our Lord.

There are different paradigms for explaining the nature of sin. It is a legal problem; we have broken God's commands. It is a relational problem; we have rejected a relationship with God. It is a spiritual problem; we have been ensnared by a spiritual enemy, Satan. It is a health problem; we have a disease that infects us and has stolen life. Regardless of the paradigm used, sin is clearly a serious issue! It should also be clear that sin is not just a behavioural issue, though it certainly reflects in our behaviour. In fact, our sin is so deep that scripture says that even our righteousness, our very best behaviour, is as filthy rags to God; even our very best efforts are tainted (Isaiah 64:6). In short, we are not good people that Jesus makes a bit better, or even bad people he makes good -- we are dead people he makes alive!

> *Humans were made to function in particular ways, with worship of the creator as the central feature, and those who turn away from worship — that is the whole human race, without a single exception — are thereby opting to seek life where it is not to be*

found, which is another way of saying that they are courting their own decay and death.[4]
— N. T. Wright

Respond

Which of the paradigms listed above do you best connect with as a way of understanding the nature of sin? Why?

Have you ever been aware of your sinfulness in the face of a Holy God? Would you be willing to ask God to show you how he views sin? If no, what fears are holding you back?

Good People

Most people consider themselves to be good people. However, when asked to define what they mean by "good," a robust definition is not forthcoming. We are not the standard of goodness, God's holiness is (Leviticus 20:26).

Leviticus 20:26

You are to be holy to me because I, the Lord, am holy

In comparison to that holiness, we are found wanting. This has the implication that we do not define what sin is — God has the final word on that. Often, we think we are good enough because we have set the standard of goodness ourselves; we have self-determined truth. This self-determining of truth is a supreme act of self-deception, in which we do not acknowledge the reality of our condition, nor deal seriously with the challenges presented by the obvious brokenness in the world around us. In essence, if none of us are the problem, why is the world such a broken and messed up place?

Sin has fractured our relationship not only with our creator God but also with one another. As we establish ourselves as our own gods and define good and truth for ourselves, we are naturally put in competition with each other. In seeking what is good or best for ourselves, the inevitable consequence is that we do that which is not best (and often damaging or disastrous) for those around us. From the very onset of sin in this world, this fractured relationship with one another has been evident as a consequence of sin (Genesis 3:12-16).

We must surrender to God as the sovereign ruler and authority in creation to determine what is good, right and pure. It is not up to us. The book of Judges teaches us this by connecting the refrain, "In those days there was no king in Israel; everyone did whatever seemed right to him," to the destructive behaviour of the Israelites. When it is up to us to determine what is true or good, tremendous harm will always be the result.

Respond

In what areas of your life do you still look to yourself to determine what is "good"? How can you begin to allow God to define what is good in every area?

Do you recognize that sin is never just isolated to an individual but always affects others? How have you seen your own sin affect your relationships?

Jesus' Coming

Thankfully, the above discussion about sin is not the end of the story. As John 3:16 teaches, God loves us and desires us to be in relationship with him. Sin is a very serious and real problem, but God desires relationship with us so much that he made a way to bring reconciliation, healing, wholeness, forgiveness and redemption to us by sending Jesus.

John 3:16

For God loved the world in this way: He gave his one and only Son, so that everyone who believes in him will not perish but have eternal life. For God did not send his Son into the world to condemn the world, but to save the world through him.

That is why Jesus is the central figure around which the entirety of scripture revolves. How did Jesus accomplish so much? We're going to find out by examining two important aspects of Jesus' coming: 1) the incarnation and 2) the historicity of Jesus.

The Incarnation

Jesus is God. As John 1 so emphatically states, he is the total, perfect and complete revelation of who God is. Incarnation literally means 'with flesh on.' Jesus humbled himself by graciously entering our world and adopting the posture of the servant. We do not have to wonder what God is like; we merely need to look at Jesus as revealed in the scriptures (Philippians 2:5-11).

In Jesus' incarnation, he demonstrated what God is like. Not just in the actions of Jesus — though God's character was emphatically revealed in the actions of Jesus — but in the very act of coming, he demonstrates his deep love for us.

Jesus' life was without sin, totally, completely and entirely in alignment with the rest of the Trinity. While the Trinity is certainly something of a mystery, so too is the nature of Jesus as fully God and fully man. Nonetheless, we are compelled to hold to this glorious mystery by the witness of his life, death and resurrection, the testimony of the scriptures and the affirmations of the church .

Historical

Acts 13:28-32

Though they found no grounds for the death sentence, they asked Pilate to have him killed. When they had carried out all that had been written about him, they took him down from the tree and put him in a tomb. But God raised him from the dead, and he appeared for many days to those who came up with him from Galilee to Jerusalem...

Jesus' historicity is of paramount importance. Jesus is not an idea but a real man who lived in the first-century Roman colony of Judea. Jesus was Jewish. He was the culmination of the promises of God that began in Genesis and were continually reaffirmed to the people of Israel throughout the Old Testament. Jesus was a real man, born of a virgin into a humble home. His life came to a brutal, gruesome and horrific end in a Roman crucifixion, the result of an unjust verdict from a proud and angry mob. He, however, did not stay dead. He rose from the dead three days later. He rose from the dead! This is a historical statement, not a religious statement. If Jesus rose from the dead, then everything changes. Without the death and resurrection of Jesus as a historical fact, we have absolutely nothing to stand on, but Jesus' death and resurrection is not a metaphor, myth or symbol but a historical event!

> *In terms of the kind of proof which historians normally accept, the case we have presented that the tomb plus appearances is what generated early Christian belief, is as watertight as one is likely to find.*[5]
> —N. T. Wright

Respond

When you look at Jesus, what does he tell you about the character of God? How does that change your understanding of God?

How does the historical nature of Jesus' death and resurrection change the way that you see Christianity?

New Kingdom

Through his birth, death and resurrection, Jesus ushered in a whole new humanity. He came to bring about the Kingdom of God (Matthew 4:17). He was establishing that God, rather than rejecting humanity, had come to redeem it and be King, once and for all. In doing so, he broke the curse of sin and death, conquered the powers of evil and darkness and paid the debt that we owe to God. It is very difficult to summarize the work of Jesus in a simple statement because he has indeed accomplished so much!

Grace

At the heart of God revealed in Jesus is grace and truth. There was nothing we could have done to restore relationship with God, but Jesus' grace made a way. This is paramount; we could not have saved ourselves, but Jesus saved us. We were saved from a position where there was absolutely nothing that we could do to save ourselves. This incredible, unfair and undeserved gift of salvation is what we mean when we refer to Jesus' grace.

Romans 5:10

For if, while we were enemies, we were reconciled to God through the death of his Son, then how much more, having been reconciled, will we be saved by his life.

Model

Jesus is our model; we continually strive to be like him. Our modelling of Jesus includes the specific details of his sacrificial life, his intimacy with the Father, his care for the vulnerable, his bold teaching, his obedience to the will of the Father and his example as a disciple-maker. Following Jesus even includes obedience to his teachings such as loving our enemies and praying for those who persecute us (Matthew 5:1-11). We are also called to structure our lives following the missional model of Jesus' life — to live as sent people who give without expecting anything in return and who walk humbly and sacrificially so that the world around us can be restored to a relationship with God. However, our role does not stop there. Not only are we called to follow Christ's model in all these ways, but we are also called to actually be models ourselves. The world around us may not have a relationship with Jesus, but they should be able to see the model of Jesus at work in us.

Respond

Based on the scriptures you read, in what ways is Jesus' Kingdom different from the culture around us?

In what ways does Jesus teaching, in Matthew 5:1-11 for example, challenge how you currently think and live?

What is one area of your life that you have intentionally allowed Jesus' teaching and life to change? How? What is one area in which you are hesitant to do that? Why?

Summary

In this session, we have covered the important and serious subject of sin. We must understand the bad news in order to fully appreciate the Good News.

- There are many paradigms for understanding the nature of sin; all of them highlight how serious it is.
- Sin goes beyond our individual decisions and affects others.
- God is the ultimate standard of what is "good," not us.
- Jesus came "in the flesh" to reveal God's character of love.

- Jesus ushered in a new kingdom that we are invited into.
- Jesus came to save us even though we were enemies of God.
- Jesus desires to be our model and teacher.

Further Scripture Reading

If you would like to read more scripture on the topics in this session, please read:

☐ Genesis 3:12-16
☐ Isaiah 64:4-7
☐ Judges 21
☐ Matthew 4:17
☐ Acts 13:28-32

Questions for My Discipler

Write down a few questions that you would like to talk about with your discipler.

Discipleship Session 3

☐ Prayer

Spend time together in prayer, invite the Holy Spirit to guide your conversation. Take a moment to sit in silence as you prepare to listen to God's leading.

☐ Celebration

What can you celebrate since you last met? How is God moving in your lives? What discipleship stories can you share?

☐ Review Previous Session

Take a moment to review the previous session. Are there any discussion points or items that you need to follow up on?

☐ Scripture

Read two passages of scripture from the ones used in the session. Choose one that encouraged and one that challenged you.

☐ God

What are the primary attributes that you learned about God's character in this section? What encouraged or challenged you?

☐ Yourself

What did you learn about yourself from the above passages?

☐ Obedience

Does what you learned change the way you think?

Does what you learned about change the way you act?

Does what you learned about change the way you treat others?

☐ Questions

Take a moment to talk through the questions you had.

☐ Next Step

What is one step you can take between now and your next session to practice what you learned?

Who can you share what you learned with to help them know Jesus?

☐ Pray

Share concerns. Pray for one another. Invite the Holy Spirit to help you.

☐ Next Discipleship Session _____

4

Response & The Holy Spirit

Welcome! In this session, we will look at the next two gospel fluency moorings; our response to Jesus and how we are filled with the Holy Spirit. Take a moment and thank Jesus that he is inviting you to know him.

Scripture Reading

To help you prepare, read the following scriptures on your own:

- ☐ Acts 2:37-38
- ☐ Romans 10:9
- ☐ Matthew 28:19
- ☐ Ephesians 1:13-14
- ☐ John 14:25-26
- ☐ 1 Corinthians 12:1-11

Respond

From the above scriptures, what kinds of responses do we have to the grace of Jesus? What role does the Holy Spirit play?

Response

Inner-Life Response

Acts 2:37-38

When they heard this, they were pierced to the heart and said to Peter and the rest of the apostles: "Brothers, what should we do?" Peter replied, "Repent and be baptized, each of you, in the name of Jesus Christ for the forgiveness of your sins, and you will receive the gift of the Holy Spirit.

As the crowds in Acts 2:37-38 show, the Gospel invites a response from us. While God's grace has been freely given to us, we must still respond. We must receive it! It is not enough to intellectually agree with the Gospel; we must respond by giving Jesus our lives.

Our response to the grace of Jesus is expressed both in our inner life and outer life. Our response begins in the inner life when we believe in our hearts that Jesus is Lord and affirm with our lips that God raised him from the dead.

Romans 10:9

If you declare with your mouth, "Jesus is Lord," and believe in your heart that God raised him from the dead, you will be saved.

We receive the new life that he has to offer and we give our lives over to him. At this point, we become recipients of his forgiveness and grace. As we are instructed in Romans 5:17, we must receive God's gift of grace. He has already offered it, so we do not need to ask for it, we merely need to receive it. Our response will include a serious repentance in our lives; we must turn from our ways and begin to chase wholeheartedly after the things of Jesus, forsaking all else and only desiring to see him glorified in us.

Outer-Life Response

Second, just as Jesus' grace was extended to us, we get the joy of extending his grace to others — this is what it means to live on mission. Part of our response to the Gospel is helping others know it as well. The Gospel compels us to be people whose lives will bear the Gospel to those who have not yet heard it. Our confession of Jesus as Lord results in a reconfiguration of our entire lives around his purpose and mission. Living a missional life is not an optional, nice-to-have component of the Gospel: it is an integral mooring of it. As recipients of the Good News, we respond by subsequently proclaiming it to others.

> For your whole duty is discharged in this, that you confess what God has done for you; and then let this be your chief aim, that you may make this known openly, and call every one to the light, whereto ye have been called. Where you see people who are ignorant, you are to direct and teach them as you have learned, namely, how a man may be saved through the virtue and power of God, and pass from darkness to light.[6]
> — Martin Luther (ca 1517)

Our response is symbolized and celebrated in the two sacraments of Baptism and Communion; which Jesus directly and expressly commanded us to follow in Matthew 28:16 and Luke 22:19. In communion, we celebrate the work of Jesus on the cross and remind ourselves of the great cost of our freedom. In baptism, we celebrate our participation and reception of that work and proclaim to others that we will follow Jesus.

Respond

Based on your reading of the scriptures above, have you responded to Jesus in the same way as the early Christians? Why or why not?

Have you believed in your heart, and said out-loud, that Jesus is Lord? How does this change the ways in which you live?

Do you view your faith as only a private issue? Do you respond to the Gospel by sharing it with others? Why or why not?

Have you been baptized? Why or why not? Talk to your discipler about taking this step of obedience if you have not.

Holy Spirit

Our response to the Gospel is made possible by the work of the Holy Spirit in us. But who exactly is the Holy Spirit? The Holy Spirit, the third person of the Trinity, plays a critical role in establishing our gospel fluency. The Holy Spirit is fully God in the same emphatic sense that Jesus is fully God: Father, Son and Spirit, all co-equal in the Trinity. The Holy Spirit is not greater or lesser than any other member of the Trinity but rather is equal in every way.

Comforter

John 14:25-26

I have spoken these things to you while I remain with you. But the Counselor, the Holy Spirit, whom the Father will send in my name, will teach you all things and remind you of everything I have told you.

Jesus introduces the Holy Spirit to comfort and guide the disciples. We are never alone because the Holy Spirit is with us, comforting and guiding us. Forming gospel fluency is ultimately a work of the Holy Spirit. We must continually invite the Holy Spirit to work in our lives and in the lives of those we wish to reach so that they will know and respond to the grace of Jesus.

Seal

The believer is filled with the Holy Spirit at the point of accepting Jesus as Lord. The Holy Spirit serves as a mark or a seal on our salvation (Ephesians 1:13-14). We belong to God, and the enemy has no claim on us. The promised eternal life that Jesus offers us is confirmed in us by the Holy Spirit. The seal of the Holy Spirit also gives us authority as we conduct ourselves as representatives of the King, Jesus.

Power

There is a separate and distinct empowering of the Holy Spirit where each believer is specifically empowered for the purposes of building and serving the church (1 Corinthians 12:1-11, Romans 12:5-8, Ephesians 4:11-13). The Holy Spirit gives a supernatural capacity to believers to glorify God, edify the church and see people know the name of Jesus. This can be expressed in prophecy, healing, words of knowledge, tongues or other supernatural spiritual activities. The supernatural move of the Holy Spirit is a natural and normal part of the New Testament and it should be a natural and normal part of our gospel fluency — not just in theory, but in practice. It is important that the power of the Holy Spirit is intrinsically tied to mission and always points to Jesus.

For many people, the supernatural move of the Holy Spirit can be intimidating because it is unfamiliar, and many of us are not used to spiritual things. However, the Holy Spirit always moves in a way that is peaceful, kind and gentle (Galatians 5:22-33). We do not need to be afraid of the Holy Spirit; instead, we should eagerly ask him to move in our lives and in the lives of those we are discipling.

Galatians 5:22-23

But the fruit of the Spirit is love, joy, peace, patience, kindness, goodness, faithfulness, gentleness, and self-control.

Respond

Which attribute (comfort, seal or power) of the Holy Spirit have you personally experienced the most? The least?

Have you invited the Holy Spirit to fill you and give you power? Why or why not? Discuss this with your discipler and pray for one another.

Do you feel like you can hear the voice of the Holy Spirit? Take a moment to sit in silence and meditate on the passages of scripture. What might the Holy Spirit be saying?

Summary

In this session, we introduced two moorings: response and the Holy Spirit. We learned the following things:

- We must respond to the Gospel by declaring and believing that Jesus is Lord.
- Our response is made public when we are baptized.
- Part of our response to Jesus is that we begin to share the Gospel with others in our life.
- We do not go through life alone; the Holy Spirit is given to give us wisdom and comfort.
- We are secure in Christ because the Holy Spirit lives in us as a seal; we do not have to wonder if God has received us.

- We have access to supernatural power through the work of the Holy Spirit. This does not have to be weird; rather, it should be peaceful and kind.

Further Scripture Reading

If you would like to read more scripture on the topics in this session, please read:

- [ ] Romans 12:3-8
- [ ] Romans 5:17
- [ ] Luke 22:14-19
- [ ] Galatians 5:16-26

Check out the Discipleship Resources on engage.liftchurch.ca for tools to help you learn how to facilitate baptism and communion.

Questions for My Discipler

Write down a few questions that you would like to talk about with your discipler.

Discipleship Session 4

☐ Prayer

Spend time together in prayer, invite the Holy Spirit to guide your conversation. Take a moment to sit in silence as you prepare to listen to God's leading.

☐ Celebration

What can you celebrate since you last met? How is God moving in your lives? What discipleship stories can you share?

☐ Review Previous Session

Take a moment to review the previous session. Are there any discussion points or items that you need to follow up on?

☐ Scripture

Read two passages of scripture from the ones used in the session. Choose one that encouraged and one that challenged you.

☐ God

What are the primary attributes that you learned about God's character in this section? What encouraged or challenged you?

☐ Yourself

What did you learn about yourself from the above passages?

☐ Obedience

Does what you learned change the way you think?

Does what you learned about change the way you act?

Does what you learned about change the way you treat others?

☐ Questions

Take a moment to talk through the questions you had.

☐ Next Step

What is one step you can take between now and your next session to practice what you learned?

Who can you share what you learned with to help them know Jesus?

☐ Pray

Share concerns. Pray for one another. Invite the Holy Spirit to help you.

☐ Next Discipleship Session _____

5
Church & New Creation

In this session, we will look at our role in the church and how God is preparing a new creation for us. Take a moment to thank Jesus that he has a role for you in the church and that he is always in control.

Scripture Reading

To help you prepare, read the following scriptures on your own:

☐ Ephesians 3:10
☐ Acts 2:37-48
☐ Matthew 5:14-16
☐ Revelation 21:1-8
☐ 2 Peter 3:13

Respond

From the above scriptures, what does the church look like and where is our ultimate hope found?

Church

After the crowds responded to the Gospel in Acts and were baptized (see sessions 3 and 4), they quickly started to live as the church. Check out Acts 2:42-48 for a description of how they lived.

Acts 2:41-42

So those who received his word were baptized, and there were added that day about three thousand souls. And they devoted themselves to the apostles' teaching and the fellowship, to the breaking of bread and the prayers.

Responding to the Gospel and receiving the Holy Spirit was never intended to be an isolated experience. All discipleship happens in the context of a relationship with other disciples. It is the collection of relationships, empowered by the Holy Spirit, that we call the church. The church is not an optional component of the Gospel. We cannot follow God alone; we need each other. The church has the job of contextualizing this glorious grace of Jesus so that every tribe, culture and nation can know and have the opportunity to respond to it.

Family

In following Jesus, we must find ourselves walking as a family with a body of local believers. Of course, walking in relationship with people is not always easy, but the job of forming gospel fluency is to remember that our participation in a local church is not optional; it is part of what it means to be a follower of Jesus. In a family, we do not need to earn our right to belong. Participation in a church family is not earned or given as a reward for performance; it is a joyful gift from Jesus to be invited to his family. However, participation in a family does come with responsibilities. These responsibilities include the need to contribute, to fulfill our unique role and responsibility, and to see Jesus glorified through us as a part of the broader family.

> *The Church exists for nothing else but to draw men into Christ, to make them little Christs. If they are not doing that then all the cathedrals, clergy, missions, sermons, even the Bible itself are simply a waste of time.*[7]
> — C.S. Lewis

Respond

Have you committed to being a part of your local church family? When things get difficult do you tend to push in or pull away from community?

What stands out to you about the way the early church lived (Acts 2:42-47)? How does it compare with your experience of church? What is one step that you can take today to begin to change the way you view and commit to church in response to this?

Mercy & Justice

Committing to one another is important because the objective of the church is ultimately to see God made known and glorified (Ephesians 3:10).

Ephesians 3:10

This is so that God's multifaceted wisdom may now be made known through the church to the rulers and authorities in the heavens.

As with discipleship, the objective of the church is the glorification and worship of the King. The church exists for the sake of the glory of God and to be a witness of him. The church is not about us!

An important responsibility of the church is to embody and reflect the heart of God in mercy and justice to the poor, vulnerable, downtrodden, orphaned, widowed, imprisoned and sick. The church must care for the orphan and the widow, the vulnerable and the oppressed. However, the church is not a generic social services agency; it is a body of believers that points to the saving grace and love of the creator God who entered a broken world to redeem it. So, we enter the world to bring hope, life and joy as well!

Matthew 5:14-16

You are the light of the world. A town built on a hill cannot be hidden. Neither do people light a lamp and put it under a bowl. Instead they put it on its stand, and it gives light to everyone in the house. In the same way, let your light shine before others, that they may see your good deeds and glorify your Father in heaven.

Respond

In your own words, what is the purpose of church? Does your experience of church line up with that?

How are you working with your church to "shine light" into dark places? What is one step you could take to be more intentional in doing that?

New Creation

As we talked about in the Jesus mooring, Jesus came to usher in a new kingdom. Scripture concludes with the glorious promise of the new creation.

2 Peter 3:13

But based on his promise, we wait for new heavens and a new earth, where righteousness dwells.

[New creation is about] the entire renewal of the cosmos in which the Christian is invited to be a participant.[8]
— N. T. Wight

Contrary to popular belief, the final destination for followers of Jesus is not heaven. Our final destination is that of a new creation where God lives in harmony with his creation as its rightful and revered King (2 Peter 3:13). The fact that the new creation is our final destination affirms that creation is a good thing! In Genesis 1 and 2, we see that we were created for relationship and creativity. In the new creation, we will get to live into that in eternity!

Jesus will return and usher in the new creation, and with it, the final judgement (Hebrews 9:28). One important component of this judgement is that not everyone will have responded by receiving the grace that Jesus has to offer. Those who have rejected the grace of Jesus will be forever separated from God; this is what we call Hell. The eternal separation from God for those who have not received the grace of Jesus is a reality that we must hold to. Jesus is the only way to salvation. There is no other way. Apart from receiving his grace, we are totally and completely lost (Revelation 20:11-15). For this reason, we must work with urgency to see people know Jesus!

> *You cannot have hopeful and responsible action without some vision for a possible future.*[9]
> — **Lesslie Newbigin**

The new creation mooring speaks to eternal hope and justice. We are reminded that we always have hope for the future: namely, that one day Jesus will restore final justice to creation. We are not simply organic matter. We do not simply return to the dust. Instead, we were created for eternal communion with the creator of the universe. No matter the brokenness of the world around us, we always have hope that Jesus will restore ultimate justice (Romans 8:22-24). The new creation mooring supplies a profound and glorious vision of the future!

Revelation 21:3-4

God's dwelling is with humanity, and he will live with them. They will be his peoples, and God himself will be with them and will be their God. He will wipe away every tear from their eyes.

Death will be no more; grief, crying, and pain will be no more, because the previous things have passed away.

Respond

Do you feel like there is always hope for the future? When you don't, how might the idea that God will bring justice give you hope?

Have you allowed the fact that there are those who do not know the hope of Jesus to give you a sense of urgency in communicating the Gospel to them? Why or why not? How can you intentionally begin (or continue) to grow and develop this sense of urgency?

Summary

In this session, we introduced the two moorings of the church and the new creation. We learned the following things:

- We cannot be Jesus' followers on our own. We need to be committed to our local church.
- The job of the church is to introduce people to Jesus and worship God, not to keep us happy.
- The church has a mandate to care for the poor, and that means we as followers of Jesus do as well.
- We always have hope because God will ultimately bring justice.
- We live as disciple-making disciples with urgency because eternity is at stake.
- We look forward to eternity in a new creation, where Jesus will be King.

Further Scripture Reading

If you would like to read more scripture on the topics in this session, please read:

- ☐ Revelation 7:9
- ☐ Ephesians 1:20-23
- ☐ Romans 8:22-24
- ☐ Hebrews 9:28
- ☐ Revelation 20:11-15
- ☐ 2 Corinthians 5:1-10

Questions for My Discipler

Write down a few questions that you would like to talk about with your discipler.

Discipleship Session 5

☐ **Prayer**

Spend time together in prayer, invite the Holy Spirit to guide your conversation. Take a moment to sit in silence as you prepare to listen to God's leading.

☐ **Celebration**

What can you celebrate since you last met? How is God moving in your lives? What discipleship stories can you share?

☐ **Review Previous Session**

Take a moment to review the previous session. Are there any discussion points or items that you need to follow up on?

☐ **Scripture**

Read two passages of scripture from the ones used in the session. Choose one that encouraged and one that challenged you.

☐ **God**

What are the primary attributes that you learned about God's character in this section? What encouraged or challenged you?

☐ **Yourself**

What did you learn about yourself from the above passages?

☐ Obedience

Does what you learned change the way you think?

Does what you learned about change the way you act?

Does what you learned about change the way you treat others?

☐ Questions

Take a moment to talk through the questions you had.

☐ Next Step

What is one step you can take between now and your next session to practice what you learned?

Who can you share what you learned with to help them know Jesus?

☐ Pray

Share concerns. Pray for one another. Invite the Holy Spirit to help you.

☐ Next Discipleship Session _____

6
Scripture

Welcome to the final session on the gospel fluency moorings. In this session, we will look at the importance of scripture in forming our identity and relationship with God.

Scripture Reading

To help you prepare, read the following scriptures on your own:

- ☐ Luke 24:44-45
- ☐ 2 Timothy 3:14-17
- ☐ Hebrews 4:12
- ☐ Psalm 119

Respond

From the above scriptures, what role does Scripture play in the life of a disciple?

What is Scripture?

What did this book mean to me during the long and weary years of solitary confinement and then for the last four years at Dachau [concentration camp]? The Word of God was simply everything to me — comfort and strength, guidance and hope, master of my days and companion of my nights, the bread which kept me from starvation and the water of life that refreshed my soul.[10]

— Martin Niemoller

The Bible is broken up into 66 books written over thousands of years that span many different literary types, including poetry, law, history, prophecy, narrative and instructional. Despite the diversity of scripture, it all tells a single, unified story that points to Jesus.

Scripture is divided into two parts: the Old Testament, which is everything leading up to Jesus, and the New Testament, which covers roughly 75 years from the birth of Jesus through the formation of the church.

From the beginning of scripture, we see that Jesus promised to bring about a solution to the problem of sin. In fact, all of scripture is pointing to Jesus in some way. Whether it is the law, the prophets, the New Testament or the Psalms, all of it is pointing to Jesus. Significant parts of the Bible can be difficult to read, but it is all powerful and helpful (2 Timothy 3:16-17). All of scripture helps us understand who we are and who Jesus is. We must learn to be moulded by all of it. We should struggle and wrestle with it, allowing it to get inside us and call us to a greater relationship with Jesus.

For example, the repeated rebellion, sin, unfaithfulness and failure of virtually every major character in the Old Testament serves to demonstrate our need for grace. However, God's character is revealed as gracious, merciful, faithful, loving and kind — especially in the face of sin! The figures in the Old Testament are all pointing forward to Jesus, whether it is Noah, Abraham, Moses, Joshua, Rahab, Job, David or Isaiah. It is all about Jesus, and it has always been about Jesus (Luke 24:44-45).

Luke 24:44-45

[Jesus] said to them, "This is what I told you while I was still with you: Everything must be fulfilled that is written about me in the Law of Moses, the Prophets and the Psalms." Then he opened their minds so they could understand the Scriptures.

Nothing in the Old Testament, is not "about [Jesus]."[11]
— **Richard Gaffin**

Respond

Do you think of scripture as a list of rules and regulations, or is it something you study to better know and understand Jesus?

Are you regularly reading scripture? If not, what is preventing you? How can implement scripture reading into your routine?

Do you regularly share scripture with those you are discipling to encourage or challenge them? What are some scriptures that you could share?

Formed by Scripture

How do we go about being formed by scripture? Scripture extends an invitation to us to be challenged, changed and formed by God. Gospel fluency goes beyond just knowledge of scripture. We can have a great deal of knowledge of scripture without it actually changing our heart. Gospel fluency invites us into a deeper relationship with scripture, one that goes beyond a set of abstract truths and allows scripture to be transformational in our lives. This means that what we believe to be true, what we desire in life and how we practically make decisions must find their home in scripture. A disciple cannot be formed in the way of Jesus without a dependency on, faith in and formation by the Word of God. Without scripture as an anchor, we will either become overwhelmed by the challenges, discouraged in the trials or swept into the currents of our culture.

Most of us are led by our emotions. As a consequence, our emotions can become the king of our lives — we do whatever feels right in the moment. However, our emotions are not the highest truth or even the most reliable source of information. Scripture is the only thing that can take that place in our lives. Instead, our emotions serve as a signal, like a dashboard indicator on our car, inviting us to turn to scripture to calibrate what we believe and feel. As the diagram below illustrates, we must not merely accept our emotions or let them make our decisions; rather, we must allow what scripture says to define truth, direct our desires and shape our decisions. How do we do that?

Our Reality Formed by Scripture

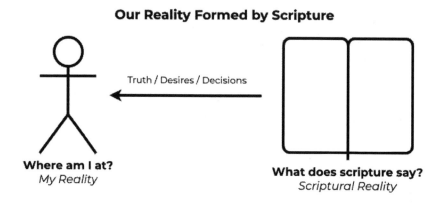

Truth / Desires / Decisions

Where am I at?
My Reality

What does scripture say?
Scriptural Reality

Scripture Defines Truth

We must first turn to scripture to define what is true. The invitation to have our reality defined by scripture applies emotionally, intellectually, morally and ethically. In our postmodern world, we have elevated the individual, as an independent moral agent, to the highest source of truth. The result of this is disastrous, as our collective sense of what is true, right and good is effectively unhinged in the process. We cannot accept or adopt an individualistic view of morality and truth. The book of Judges is a narrative account of what happens when people reject the authority of God in their lives; in short, chaos and pain ensues. We need an anchor, and that anchor is the Word of God.

Psalm 119 is the longest Psalm in scripture, and it is all about being shaped by God's Word! Knowing and obeying the Word of God enables us to walk blameless lives (verse 1). Verse 147 invites us to know the Word as our source of hope. Verse 28 beautifully states that in our grief, we can actually be strengthened by the Word!

Psalm 119

1 How happy are those whose way is blameless, who walk according to the Lord's instruction!
28 I am weary from grief; strengthen me through your word.
147 I rise before dawn and cry out for help; I put my hope in your word.

Oftentimes, there can be a difference between what we feel to be true and what scripture declares to be true. These moments can be difficult, even painful, for us to navigate. However, we must allow ourselves to be challenged by the Word and to have our lives moulded by it.

We must train our minds and hearts to yearn for and submit to scripture. Such a thing is no small task and must be an intentional act of discipleship where we ask our disciplers to train us to be formed by scripture (Ephesians 6:17).

Respond

In what areas of your life are you allowing emotion to dictate what you believe to be true? Is there an emotion, perhaps shame, neglect, anger or pride, that the scriptures could speak to in a way that would change you?

Which influences have a greater impact on your life than scripture? Is scripture the final authority or just good advice?

Do you have a habit of spending time in the Word on a daily basis as Psalm 119:147 suggests? Discuss this with your discipler.

Scripture Shapes Our Desires

As scripture begins to define what is true, right and good, it will also begin to inform the desires and longings of our soul. Perhaps the greatest challenge in the life of the disciple is keeping our desires anchored in the hope of Jesus. There are so many options that we are presented with every day that if we are not anchored in the Word, we will simply desire that which affords us the most gratification in the most expedient fashion.

In many cases, the life and work of discipleship is slow and the reward is delayed. Consequently, we must continually return to scripture to inform and shape our longings so that we are not blown off track. Philippians 2:13 beautifully says that God will give us the desire and the power to do what pleases him. Through God's word, we can see our desires moulded and shaped such that they will honour the Lord.

Philippians 2:13

For it is God who is working in you both to will and to work according to his good purpose.

That is why the real problem of the Christian life comes where people do not usually look for it. It comes the very moment you wake up each morning. All your wishes and hopes for the day rush at you like wild animals. And the first job each morning consists simply in shoving them all back; in listening to that other voice, taking that other point of view and letting that other, larger, stronger, quieter life come flowing in.[12]
— C.S. Lewis

The culture we find ourselves in is constantly vying and competing for our attention. We cannot fight the pressure of our culture on our own. It is not enough to simply force ourselves by the power of our will to be hungry for the things of God. Instead, we must continually go to scripture to inform our desires, to help create a longing for Jesus and his word. As we do that, the allure of fancy experiences or successes will fade as we begin to develop a deeper hunger for the values of Jesus: serving the poor and vulnerable, proclaiming the Gospel, worshiping the King and creating beautiful things. We will begin to see in us a genuine love for those we previously had never even considered. When the object of our affection is Jesus, we will naturally find ourselves longing for that which will best draw us into relationship with him and afford him glory.

Again, Psalm 119 invites us to treasure God's Word so that we might not desire sin (verse 11). It reminds us that our home is ultimately not this world, so we ought not to capitulate to culture (verse 19), and it reminds us to delight in the Word and, in so doing, be directed by it (verse 24).

Psalm 119

11 I have treasured your word in my heart so that I may not sin against you.
19 I am a resident alien on earth; do not hide your commands from me.
24 your decrees are my delight and my counsellors.

Part of discipleship is learning to have our desires align with the desires of Jesus. We must genuinely and thoroughly desire to see the Kingdom of God on earth as it is in heaven. Jesus' instruction to pray for his Kingdom was an instruction to see the purposes of God completely and totally formed in us. We must be willing to challenge those we are discipling when they begin to express desires for things that are not of Jesus. We must call them back to be formed by the Word before they drift into a general apathy towards the mission of Christ.

Respond

Identify a passage of scripture that you already know. What would change in your life if you honestly allowed this passage to truly shape your desires, hopes and dreams? (If you can't think of one, check out Matthew 5:1-11.)

Are there things that you are craving that scripture would invite you to think differently about? For example, a relationship or job?

Scripture Directs our Decisions

As scripture lays the foundation of truth and shapes our desires, it must also direct our decisions. The Psalmist writes that his direction actually changed as a result of scripture (verse 59) and that scripture served as his guide on how to navigate the future (verse 105).

Psalm 119

59 I thought about my ways and turned my steps back to your decrees.
105 Your word is a lamp for my feet and a light on my path.

While scripture informs what is true, and even directs our desires, it is when our decisions are actually shaped by scripture that the true power of the Word is unlocked. When what we believe, what we desire and what we do are all rooted in scripture, there is tremendous joy.

Scripture calls us to love our enemies and pray for those who persecute us. When we actually start to love our enemies and forgive those who have hurt us, the power of scripture becomes real to us. It is not enough to agree with scripture; we must actually do what it says. However, the life that scripture invites us into is tremendously challenging. The call to forgiveness, mission, sacrifice, love and endurance that the Word extends to us is totally contrary to our human nature and is incredibly difficult.

A mark of a mature Christian is that they can hear, read and study scripture on their own and allow the Holy Spirit to convict them in areas of their life that are not yet surrendered. Many Christians are rich in knowledge and poor in execution. They may agree with scripture, but their actual decisions are hardly informed by it. Invite your discipler to challenge you with scripture in your life (1 Peter 2:2-3).

Part of being a multiplying disciple is to develop a missional framework for decision making. This means that the way we make decisions is informed by scripture with the goal being to maximize the glory of God in our lives. Our world offers many competing frameworks for making decisions, such as maximizing comfort, wealth, fame or experiences. We must invite the people we are discipling to build a framework for decision making that forsakes comfort, wealth, fame or any other worldly venture and instead seeks to see decisions made with Jesus' glory as the goal. Such a missional proposition is only possible if our worldview is completely saturated with the words of scripture.

Hebrews 4:12

For the word of God is living and effective and sharper than any double-edged sword, penetrating as far as the separation of soul and spirit, joints and marrow. It is able to judge the thoughts and intentions of the heart.

Respond

Study Psalm 119:28,59,105,130,142,147 - how do your current patterns of thinking and beliefs align with those truths?

When you make major decisions, do you use scripture as a primary guide in the process? What is one decision you have to make that you and your discipler can apply scripture to?

Summary

In this session, we discussed the importance of scripture in developing our gospel fluency. We specifically learned:

- The importance of daily time in scripture.
- The way that scripture defines what is true.
- All of scripture points to Jesus and helps us know God's character.
- Scripture shapes our desires to be more like Jesus.
- Scripture gives wisdom so that we can make decisions that glorify God.

Further Scripture Reading

If you would like to read more scripture on the topics in this session, please read:

- ☐ 1 Peter 2:2-3
- ☐ Ephesians 6:17
- ☐ Romans 8

Check out *BibleProject* (thebibleproject.com) online for fantastic resources to help you study scripture.

Check out the Discipleship Resources on engage.liftchurch.ca for tools to help you develop gospel fluency.

Questions for My Discipler

Write down a few questions that you would like to talk about with your discipler.

Discipleship Session 6

☐ Prayer

Spend time together in prayer, invite the Holy Spirit to guide your conversation. Take a moment to sit in silence as you prepare to listen to God's leading.

☐ Celebration

What can you celebrate since you last met? How is God moving in your lives? What discipleship stories can you share?

☐ Review Previous Session

Take a moment to review the previous session. Are there any discussion points or items that you need to follow up on?

☐ Scripture

Read two passages of scripture from the ones used in the session. Choose one that encouraged and one that challenged you.

☐ God

What are the primary attributes that you learned about God's character in this section? What encouraged or challenged you?

☐ Yourself

What did you learn about yourself from the above passages?

☐ Obedience

Does what you learned change the way you think?

Does what you learned about change the way you act?

Does what you learned about change the way you treat others?

☐ Questions

Take a moment to talk through the questions you had.

☐ Next Step

What is one step you can take between now and your next session to practice what you learned?

Who can you share what you learned with to help them know Jesus?

☐ Pray

Share concerns. Pray for one another. Invite the Holy Spirit to help you.

☐ Next Discipleship Session _____

7

Confession, Meditation & Repentance

Welcome to the final session focused on developing your gospel fluency. In this session, we will apply the spiritual practices of confession, meditation and repentance to help you better walk with Jesus.

Scripture Reading

To help you prepare, read the following scriptures on your own:

- [ ] Deuteronomy 6:6-9
- [ ] Psalm 51
- [ ] 1 Peter 3:15
- [ ] Romans 8:37-38

Respond

When you think of confession, meditation and repentance, do you think of life-giving or life-draining activities? Why is that?

Practicing Gospel Fluency

The understanding that gospel fluency involves truth, desires and decisions is of paramount importance. How do we practically allow scripture to take such a prominent place in our lives? What are the tools, methods and techniques that we can use to see scripture form our understanding of what is true, our desires and our decisions?

When God gave his word to the Israelites, he gave them a set of commands in Deuteronomy 6 so that the nation would be formed by God's word. These commands came to be known as *The Shema* and were often repeated as part of daily prayer by ancient Israelites. From this command, we find three powerful actions that we can take towards this end: meditation, confession and repentance.

Deuteronomy 6:6-9

These words that I am giving you today are to be in your heart. Repeat them to your children. Talk about them when you sit in your house and when you walk along the road, when you lie down and when you get up. Bind them as a sign on your hand and let them be a symbol on your forehead. Write them on the doorposts of your house and on your city gates.

Meditation

6 These words that I am giving you today are to be in your heart.

The first tool is that of meditation. Biblical meditation is the process of filling our thoughts with the words of scripture, allowing scripture to be impressed upon our minds and hearts.

For many people, when they think of meditation, it is a process of "emptying" the mind — not thinking about anything. That is not the Biblical conception of meditation. Biblical meditation is all about filling our minds with the truths of God's word. It is essentially the opposite. Ajith Fernando, in his book *The Call to Joy and Pain*, calls this process "preaching to our heart."

> *Because our heart is struggling with the situation, our mind preaches to the heart the truths we know from the Word.... We must learn to stop listening to our self-pitying conversation and start preaching the deeper realities to ourselves.*[13]
> — Ajith Fernando

Three practices to assist our meditation on scripture are memorization, devotions and praying scripture.

First, we develop in ourselves, and others, the habit of memorizing scripture so that we can recall it throughout the day. We cannot effectively be formed by scripture, or disciple others, unless we have a robust knowledge of the word. In order to be making decisions, managing our emotions and discerning what is true on a day-to-day basis, we must have a deep familiarity with scripture.

1 Peter 3:15

In your hearts regard Christ the Lord as holy, ready at any time to give a defense to anyone who asks you for a reason for the hope that is in you.

To both adequately explain our faith to those who do not know Jesus and raise disciples ourselves, we need to know what the Bible says. Memorizing scripture is a crucial aspect of this sort of preparation.

Second, we must have the habit of turning daily to the scriptures in moments of quiet and calm. It is in our devotions that we intentionally create space to fill our thoughts with scripture and allow them to take root in us. To effectively meditate on scripture, we must remove distractions and allow all of our attention to centre on scripture.

Third, we can develop the practice of praying scripture over ourselves and others. For example, Psalm 51 contains beautiful truths about our sinfulness being met by the grace of God. As Romans 8 describes God's love for us, we should not just dwell on it but actually form it into our prayers. That means that we can take the words and use them as prayers instead of our own words.

Respond

Take a moment to memorize Romans 8:37-38. Write it out below to help you develop the habit.

In the last session, and again in this session, we talked about the need for daily devotions. Have you been developing a habit of reading scripture? What is working? What are you struggling with?

What is one piece of scripture that you have meditated on that you can share with someone you hope to disciple or lead to Jesus?

Confession

Deuteronomy 6:7

Repeat them to your children. Talk about them when you sit in your house and when you walk along the road, when you lie down and when you get up.

The formation of scripture in our lives is not an individual pursuit; rather, it is one that is done in the context of discipleship relationships and our broader church family. As we study and are convicted by scripture in our times of meditation or through the coaching of the person who is discipling us, we must reach a point where we are ready to confess that we need to change.

Confession comes from the Greek word *homologeo,* which literally means "to say the same thing." Biblical confession is not *just* about admitting or acknowledging sin. It is actually a process where we begin to declare that what scripture says is true! Confession is a process where we bring our thoughts and desires into alignment with scripture. When confessing sin, we acknowledge that we have offended God's holiness. However, as we study the scriptures describing God's love for us, we can also confess that over ourselves or others. As we confess God's love for us to another person, we begin to be moulded and shaped by it.

In confession, we begin to declare that which is true about God and about us. Confession is not a dull, dreary or depressing act. Rather, it is sublime in that through confession, we begin to declare the freeing truth of God's word over our lives. Confession is one of the most life-giving and liberating things we can do.

It is for this reason that being formed by scripture is actually a matter of discipleship, not just individual faith. When we invite those we are discipling to confess the truth of scripture, we are doing some of the most important and powerful discipleship work we can do.

Again in Psalm 51, we see David, the Psalmist, confessing his sin to God after he was confronted about it by the prophet Nathan. David recognizes the serious nature of his actions and seeks the Lord's forgiveness. Thankfully, the psalm does not end on a sour or depressing note. Rather, we see David beginning to experience the joy and freedom that comes from being honest with others and God through confession.

Respond

What has been your experience of confession thus far in your life? Were you met with grace or judgement?

Remember that regardless of your previous experiences, Jesus offers you forgiveness of your sin rather than condemnation as you come to him.

Do you struggle to confess your sins to Jesus? Why or why not? Take a moment to pause and reflect on your answer. Invite the Holy Spirit to speak to you.

Is there anything that scripture has specifically revealed that you need to confess? Take a moment now and confess it to God and later to your discipler.

Repentance

Deuteronomy 6:8-9

Bind them as a sign on your hand and let them be a symbol on your forehead. Write them on the doorposts of your house and on your city gates.

Repentance is about changing direction. When we repent, we are allowing scripture to serve as a directional guide for us. It is when we acknowledge that we need to change our behaviour and go in a different direction that we unlock the real power of scripture. As with confession, repentance is about more than simply dealing with sin. Yes, much of repentance will have to do with sin and behaviour. But we should also repent when we have allowed ourselves to believe and act according to things that are untrue. For example, when we meditate on the truth that we are loved by God and confess that over ourselves as true, we must begin to act according to that truth — that is repentance. In repentance, our beliefs, words and actions find themselves in alignment.

Matthew 4:17

From then on Jesus began to preach, "Repent, because the kingdom of heaven has come near."

Repentance should be a daily action taken by the disciple. We must daily call the people we are discipling to repent: to turn around and bring their actions into alignment with scripture. The daily decision to take specific actions to allow our lives to be moulded by scripture is a powerful act, but one that we must develop as a habit — both in ourselves and in those we are discipling.

Finally, it must be clearly said, repentance flows from the fact that we are first loved by God. Our repentance is not an action taken to earn the love of God; rather, it is an action taken because we already have the love of God!

Respond

Do you view the call to repentance as a negative, fearful obligation or a life-giving, freeing gift?

Is there any area of your life right now where you need to turn around and go in a new, Jesus focused, direction? Good places to check include relationships, career, recreational activities or finances.

> *I have wanted to make people aware and to admit that I find the New Testament very easy to understand, but thus far I have found it tremendously difficult to act literally upon what it so plainly says.*[14]
> — Soren Kierkegaard

Summary

The diagram below illustrates how the three actions of meditation, confession and repentance initiate a cycle whereby scripture can be formational in our desires, emotions and decisions.

Formed By Scripture Through Spiritual Practices

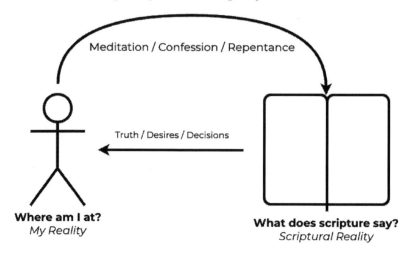

Meditation / Confession / Repentance

Truth / Desires / Decisions

Where am I at?
My Reality

What does scripture say?
Scriptural Reality

It should be apparent that gospel fluency is so much deeper than knowledge! While knowledge is important, true gospel fluency is about the total transformation of our heart, mind and actions to align with the life-giving joy that is described in the scriptures. Through meditation, confession and repentance, we can be truly and thoroughly formed by scripture. In this session, we:

- Reaffirmed the importance of daily time in Scripture.
- Highlighted the importance of scripture memorization.
- Gained some valuable tools for meditating biblically.
- Learned that confession is about recognizing how God sees things.
- Discovered how life-giving repentance can be.

Further Scripture Reading

If you would like to read more scripture on the topics in this session, please read:

☐ Psalm 51

Check out the Discipleship Resources on engage.liftchurch.ca for tools to help you develop gospel fluency.

Questions for My Discipler

Write down a few questions that you would like to talk about with your discipler.

Discipleship Session 7

☐ Prayer

Spend time together in prayer, invite the Holy Spirit to guide your conversation. Take a moment to sit in silence as you prepare to listen to God's leading.

☐ Celebration

What can you celebrate since you last met? How is God moving in your lives? What discipleship stories can you share?

☐ Review Previous Session

Take a moment to review the previous session. Are there any discussion points or items that you need to follow up on?

☐ Scripture

Read two passages of scripture from the ones used in the session. Choose one that encouraged and one that challenged you.

☐ God

What are the primary attributes that you learned about God's character in this section? What encouraged or challenged you?

☐ Yourself

What did you learn about yourself from the above passages?

☐ Obedience

Does what you learned change the way you think?

Does what you learned about change the way you act?

Does what you learned about change the way you treat others?

☐ Questions

Take a moment to talk through the questions you had.

☐ Next Step

What is one step you can take between now and your next session to practice what you learned?

Who can you share what you learned with to help them know Jesus?

☐ Pray

Share concerns. Pray for one another. Invite the Holy Spirit to help you.

☐ Next Discipleship Session _____

Part 2

Secure Identity

8

Jesus as Lord

Welcome to your eighth discipleship session. This will be the first of four sessions that focus specifically on the secure identity discipleship emphasis. Take a moment to praise God for the work he is already doing in your life and, through you, in others'.

Scripture Reading

To help you prepare, read the following scriptures on your own:

- ☐ Romans 1:21-23
- ☐ Ephesians 2:4-5
- ☐ Colossians 3:1-17
- ☐ Romans 6:1-13

Respond

From the scriptures above, who are you before Jesus? What about after Jesus' work in your life?

Secure Identity

A secure identity, in light of the glorious hope found in the Gospel, is the second emphasis in developing discipleship potential. Secure identity is the discipleship emphasis that involves our reception of Jesus as Lord and our formation as children, servants and ambassadors of God.

In speaking of secure identity, we aim to get to the heart of the question, "Who am I?" The answer to this question is foundational to informing our perspective of the role we play in the Kingdom of Jesus, and it profoundly influences our behaviour, relationships, vocation and virtually every other aspect of our lives. When we can clearly and confidently identify who we are, we become far more effective as multiplying disciples. The question is, who are we?

Jesus as Lord

The foundational starting place for discussing a secure identity is the Gospel itself. We start with who we are by first understanding and positioning ourselves in relationship to the Creator God of the universe. As we say sometimes, "There is a God, and it's not you." The Gospel tells us there is a God who cares profoundly about his creation. He is creative, involved, kind, loving and merciful. We cannot correctly understand who we are until we first surrender to who God is. The need to position ourselves in relationship to the Creator God is why Jesus says in John 3:16 that whoever believes in him will have eternal life, and why Paul says in Romans 10:9 that if we confess with our mouth that Jesus is Lord, we will be saved. The starting point for understanding who we are is understanding and surrendering to who God is. Everything about who we are is in response to who God is. This recognition of who Jesus is, and his rightful place as Lord of our lives, is perhaps one of the most significant barriers to people accepting the Gospel. To acknowledge who Jesus is, we must implicitly also recognize who we are in relation to him — a position that fundamentally requires that we surrender our rights and responsibilities — he is God and we are not!

It is absolutely crucial that we emphasize the necessity of Jesus as Lord, as our human propensity is to do precisely the opposite. Rather than allowing Jesus to be Lord over every area of our lives, we tend to manufacture God into our own image (Romans 1:21-23).

Romans 1:21-23

For though they knew God, they did not glorify him as God or show gratitude. Instead, their thinking became worthless, and their senseless hearts were darkened. Claiming to be wise, they became fools and exchanged the glory of the immortal God for images resembling mortal man

Rather than allowing God to inform, direct and establish what is true, we instead build for ourselves an understanding of God that affirms who we already think we are. If we are angry, then God is angry. If we are vengeful, then God must be vengeful. If we are greedy, then we imagine God affirming our greediness. If we are lustful, we look for God to affirm our lust. Our vision of God can end up as a reflection of us to such an extent that the God of the scriptures and our personal understanding of him are worlds apart.

It might appear that this discussion belongs under Gospel Fluency, but it is placed here because only when Jesus is Lord can we truly be secure in who we are. Our security in Jesus is not possible as long as we continue to live as Lord of our lives. Only when Jesus informs who we are do we gain the footing for a bold and vibrant life. To say that this is counter to our nature is an understatement. In our pride and sin, we cling to our lives under the illusion that we are in control. However, nothing could be further from the truth. It is only in surrender to Jesus that we can indeed be secure, because it is only he who is truly in control (Matthew 10:39). Consequently, a secure identity without a proper understanding of Jesus' lordship is simply not possible. That is why Romans 1 goes on to describe the sheer and utter lostness in humanity that comes from a refusal to surrender.

When the frontier between God and Man is not closed, the barrier between what is normal and what is perverse is opened.[15]
— **Karl Barth**

Respond

Why is it so important that we start with Jesus as Lord when answering the question, "Who am I?"

Take a moment and pray. What are the areas of your life where you are still "lord" or in control? Ask Jesus to help you to surrender them to him.

Fully Alive

To form a secure identity, we must first surrender to Jesus as Lord. It is through surrendering that we begin to experience a total transformation into who he created us to be. We find our new identity in Christ through acceptance of his gift of new life. The transformation that occurs through this acceptance and surrender is what it means to be fully alive in the hope of Jesus. As a result, understanding that we are fully alive is the starting point for developing a secure identity. Without Jesus we are not just bad, lost, orphaned or alone, we are dead. However, because of the grace of Jesus, we find ourselves fully alive.

Ephesians 2:4-5

But God, who is rich in mercy, because of his great love that he had for us, made us alive with Christ even though we were dead in trespasses. You are saved by grace!

This change in identity, from 'dead' to 'alive,' leads to a transformation in both our inner life as well as our outer life. If we are now alive because of Jesus, then every aspect of our lives will align behind that reality. Our behaviour, lifestyle and decisions are often a direct consequence of what we perceive our identity to be. Behaviour and lifestyle decisions are an identity issue! As Colossians 3 puts it, our new identity is that of being alive in Christ, which means that we must "put to death" the things of this world. Our behaviour, or our misbehaviour, is directly related to the depth of our 'fully alive' identity in Jesus

Colossians 3:1,5

So if you have been raised with Christ, seek the things above... put to death what belongs to your earthly nature

Paul goes on in Colossians to highlight a host of different components of a life that is not fully alive: sexual immorality, idolatry, rage, anger, greed and so forth. Paul's invitation is great news because it means that the solution to the unhealth in our inner life is to press more deeply into the things of Jesus — or as Paul says, to "set our eyes on things above." The message of Jesus is not, "stop doing these things." Rather, the message is, "turn around, I have a better way for you to live!" Paul reiterates this with great precision in Romans 6:11:

Romans 6:11

Consider yourselves dead to sin and alive to God in Christ Jesus.

Paul's instruction that we should "consider ourselves alive" means that we must forge an identity, and an understanding of who we are, that is built upon the fact that we are fully alive in Jesus.

This transformation is not merely in our inner life (our behaviour, thoughts and actions); but equally applies to our outer life — our ability to be disciple-making disciples. After Paul's instruction to put to death our sinful nature and put on our life in Christ, he commands the church to adopt a different way of living, filled with compassion, grace and love. His invitation to a fully alive identity culminates in the following multiplication-oriented command in verse 17:

Colossians 3:17

Whatever you do, in word or in deed, do everything in the name of the Lord Jesus, giving thanks to God the Father through him.

When we start to live fully alive, every aspect of our lives begins to be used and leveraged for the Glory of Jesus. It is from our transformed identities that we discover Kingdom effectiveness, as Romans 6 highlights.

Romans 6:13

But as those who are alive from the dead, offer yourselves to God, and all the parts of yourselves to God as weapons for right-eousness.

Weapons of righteousness is a powerful and vivid picture of a church on the offensive! When we have built our identity upon the fact that we are fully alive in Christ, we will inevitably see both inner-life and outer-life transformation. The offence here is not an offence of violence but one of a weapon of truth. In Revelation 19:15, Jesus is depicted with a sword proceeding from his mouth as he overthrows the powers of darkness. It is the words of Jesus, the truth proclaimed, that is his most powerful weapon. The weapon that Jesus wields is ultimately not a physical weapon but a spiritual one: a weapon of truth. The dual-sided truth that we are dead in our sins, but because of the grace of Jesus, we have been declared righteous, is a powerful testimony on which we build our lives. Indeed, by the grace of Jesus, we have been raised from death to life, and the effect should be noticeable in such a way to the world around us that they desire to know Jesus as well. We do not need to live timid, afraid or ashamed, but rather we live as a people who have been assigned a glorious mission of seeing the world around us set free by the grace and goodness of Jesus. As we have been raised to life by Jesus, the testimony of our lives becomes a weapon to see others equally set free.

Respond

Which parts of the way that you currently live are reflective of your old identity before Christ? (Use Colossians 3 as a guide.) Which parts of your life are reflective of your new identity since you have been made fully alive in Christ?

What does it mean that you are a weapon of righteousness? From your answer, how could you live in a way so that other people can also be fully alive in Jesus?

New Identities

With our identity securely built upon being fully alive in the hope of Jesus, we can turn our attention to several other essential identity markers that are integral to a secure identity in Christ. In Christ, we have the following identities, to list just a few:

- A priest (1 Peter 2:9)
- New creation (2 Corinthians 5:17)
- Righteous (2 Corinthians 5:21)
- Light of the world (Matthew 5:14)
- Salt of the earth (Matthew 5:13)
- Friend of God (John 15:15)
- Forgiven (Romans 5:1)
- Son or daughter (Galatians 3:26)
- Heir with Christ (Romans 8:17)
- More than a conqueror (Romans 8:37)
- Temple for the Holy Spirit (1 Corinthians 3:16)
- A saint (Philippians 1:1)
- Chosen (Ephesians 1:4)
- A citizen of heaven (Philipians 3:20)
- Alien or stranger in the world (1 Peter 2:11)
- Redeemed (Revelation 5:9)

We are going to specifically focus on three of the identities we have in Christ: a child of God, an ambassador for the Kingdom of God and, lastly, a slave/servant of Jesus. These are our relational, missional and sacrificial identities in Christ. These will be discussed in detail in the following chapters.

Secure Identities

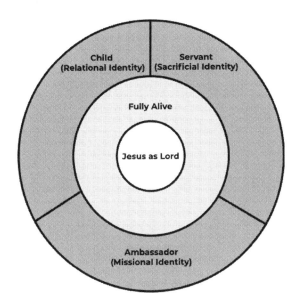

Respond

Which of the identities listed above do you feel you believe to be true about yourself? Which one is the most encouraging to hear about, and why?

Which of the identities listed above can you remind someone in your life about to encourage them as they also follow Jesus?

Summary

We discussed how our new identity in Christ paves the way for a life of freedom and joy as well as multiplication effectiveness. We specifically discussed:

- The starting place for our secure identity in Christ is recognizing him as Lord of our lives.
- Many of our sinful or hurtful behaviour flows from parts of our lives where Jesus is not Lord.
- When we recognize Jesus as Lord, the primary identity we receive is that we have been made fully alive.
- We are called to live as "weapons of righteousness" in leading other people to know Jesus.
- There are many glorious and beautiful identities that Christ gives us.

Further Scripture Reading

If you would like to read more scripture on the topics in this session, please read:

- ☐ Revelation 19:15
- ☐ Matthew 10:39

Questions for My Discipler

Write down a few questions that you would like to talk about with your discipler.

Discipleship Session 8

☐ **Prayer**

Spend time together in prayer, invite the Holy Spirit to guide your conversation. Take a moment to sit in silence as you prepare to listen to God's leading.

☐ **Celebration**

What can you celebrate since you last met? How is God moving in your lives? What discipleship stories can you share?

☐ **Review Previous Session**

Take a moment to review the previous session. Are there any discussion points or items that you need to follow up on?

☐ **Scripture**

Read two passages of scripture from the ones used in the session. Choose one that encouraged and one that challenged you.

☐ **God**

What are the primary attributes that you learned about God's character in this section? What encouraged or challenged you?

☐ **Yourself**

What did you learn about yourself from the above passages?

☐ Obedience

Does what you learned change the way you think?

Does what you learned about change the way you act?

Does what you learned about change the way you treat others?

☐ Questions

Take a moment to talk through the questions you had.

☐ Next Step

What is one step you can take between now and your next session to practice what you learned?

Who can you share what you learned with to help them know Jesus?

☐ Pray

Share concerns. Pray for one another. Invite the Holy Spirit to help you.

☐ Next Discipleship Session _____

9
Child

This is the second session that will focus on secure identity, specifically the relational identity of a child. Pause for a second and thank God that you are fully alive in him as you read the scriptures below.

Scripture Reading

To help you prepare, read the following scriptures on your own:

- ☐ Ephesians 1:5
- ☐ Galatians 5:4-6
- ☐ 1 John 3:1
- ☐ Ephesians 2:19
- ☐ Hebrews 10:25
- ☐ Hebrews 13:17

Respond

From the scriptures above , what does it mean to you that you are a Child of God? Is that a comforting idea? Why or why not?

Child — Relational Identity

One of the most beautiful truths that we discover as we become fully alive is that we find ourselves adopted as sons and daughters of God. In the Old Testament, God initially chose a nation for himself in Abraham and the subsequent nation of Israel (see Genesis 12). However, God's ultimate purpose was that, through

Abraham, someone would come who would see all people adopted into the family of God. The promises to Abraham ultimately culminated in the work of Jesus. It is through the work of Jesus that our adoption as sons and daughters is made possible:

Galatians 4:5-6

And because you are sons, God sent the Spirit of his Son into our hearts, crying, "Abba, Father!" So you are no longer a slave but a son, and if a son, then God has made you an heir.

1 John 3:1

See what great love the Father has given us that we should be called God's children—and we are!

Jesus graciously made our inclusion in his family possible through his death and resurrection. Perhaps the most incredible aspect of our adoption is that it was always a part of God's eternal plan!

When the writer of Ephesians describes how God predestined us to be adopted, it is a reference to God's ultimate purpose for humanity (Ephesians 1:5). His purpose, from before the creation of the world, was that we would be adopted as sons and daughters in Jesus. Our adoption was not an afterthought or simply something that is nice to have. God created us to be sons and daughters through the blood of Jesus. Moreover, God delights in our adoption; it brings him joy when we turn to him. God is not satisfied or delighted in our performance; rather, he is delighted when we receive his gift of life in Jesus. His love for us is completely independent of our performance, as it was ultimately Jesus who made it possible, not us.

Respond

Has your upbringing allowed you to see God as an unconditionally loving Father? Why or why not? Is this a helpful or a difficult truth for you to believe?

Do you feel like anything from your past separates you from the love of God? Pause and reflect. Write down some of the thoughts that come to mind. Ask your discipler to pray with you to know that God is overjoyed when we come to him.

Applying our Identity

Our adoption has two immediate applications: one to our inner life and one to our outer life. First, as sons and daughters, we are secure in the fact that there is nothing we can do to earn God's love and, by extension, nothing we can do to lose his love. Nothing in all creation can ever separate us from his love (Romans 8:39). Our security in God's love frees us from a performance-oriented relationship with God. We do not need to earn his love or his favour because he has already freely given it to us! In a culture where acceptance has a direct correlation to performance, this is a radical truth!

Romans 8:38-39

For I am persuaded that neither death nor life, nor angels nor rulers, nor things present nor things to come, nor powers, nor height nor depth, nor any other created thing will be able to separate us from the love of God that is in Christ Jesus our Lord.

Many of us live with an attitude of lack or deficiency and live our lives with the belief that we are victims or defeated. While we may tragically be the victims of the sin of others, and may suffer setbacks, our identity in Christ gives us the joy of a greater promise: that we are secure in Jesus! In fact, all of the promises that the Lord gave to Abraham (being a blessing to the nations) are ours in Christ (Galatians 3:14). As sons and daughters of God, we get to share in Jesus' glory. While this will likely involve trials and suffering, we can always remain firm and secure in the promise of Jesus' goodness (Romans 8:17). Jesus, likewise, promised that our Father would take care of us:

Matthew 7:11

If you then, who are evil, know how to give good gifts to your children, how much more will your Father in heaven give good things to those who ask him.

Second, if God's love is free and utterly independent from what we have done, that kind of love will change the way we see and interact with others in the world around us. It is only natural that as we learn to be secure in the fact that God loves us as sons and daughters, we will desire to see those in the world around us discover that kind of love as well. A person secure in the love of God will naturally lead those around them to also be secure in the love of God. The fact that God desires to see those we are reaching adopted as sons and daughters is the driving force behind the "Everyone" in 'Everyone Sent to Multiply Everything.' When we learn to view people through a lens that allows us to see them adopted as sons and daughters, we will inevitably learn to see them for the tremendous value that they actually have.

Respond

Do you operate out of a mindset of poverty (financially, relationally or otherwise)? How does knowing that you have a good Father who loves to bless you speak to that?

Are you discipling people to be secure in their identity in Christ themselves? Is the way that you love people, especially those not like you or those that you do not have good "chemistry" with, leading them to know the love of Jesus? How so or why not?

Secure in Church Family

When thinking about forming an identity, many of us tend to think of it as an individual pursuit. We tend to think of how we can be secure without any consideration of the broader community in which we find ourselves. Our self-centred, individualistic propensity for identity formation is nothing short of disastrous for the Kingdom of God and is one of the largest barriers for discipleship.

We live in a world where faith is a largely private affair and the role of community is discounted or ignored. However, we are no longer alone on our journey but find ourselves as a part of a family as expressed in the form of a local church. If we are sons and daughters in Christ, then we are equally brothers and sisters in Christ!

> *We belong to each other because we share a heavenly Father. Our identity and our calling must emanate from God's image radiating in and through us.*[16]
> — Rosaria Butterfield

The connection between the local church and our adoption as sons and daughters in Christ is essential. These theological concepts are intimately intertwined. It is in the church family that our security in Christ finds a context to be realized. This concept is explicitly stated in Ephesians 2:19:

Ephesians 2:19

So then you are no longer foreigners and strangers, but fellow citizens with the saints, and members of God's household

When we submit to one another in the context of church family, we are actually reenacting the Gospel itself. Just as Christ died for us, we get the joy of laying down our lives for one another (Ephesians 5:15-33).

It is in the church that we learn to love the unlovable, forgive the unforgivable and walk in unity despite hurt and pain — all things that Christ has done for us (Colossians 3:13)! We are not easily offended because we know that without Christ, we are offensive to God and therefore are dependent on his grace. As recipients of grace, we are eager to extend grace and, in so doing, see Christ formed in us and others. It is in the church that we learn to receive Christ's love for us as we give it to, and receive it from, others. Without the application of the Gospel to our brothers and sisters in Christ, our true security in Christ will never be formed in us.

Perpetua & Friends - 3rd Century Martyr
Perpetua was executed in a Roman gladiatorial ring alongside five others. What is notable is that the others were both slaves and free men. Two slaves, three free men and noblewomen were brutally martyred as family. Despite hailing from vastly different backgrounds and finding themselves in a very hopeless situation, they were full of joy as they prepared to die for their faith. Multiple times in the account of their death, they praise the Lord that they are together as brothers and sisters. The fact that they were totally secure as sons and daughters of Christ as they faced death is no doubt also connected to their intimate connection as brothers and sisters in the faith.

We cannot be secure as sons and daughters in Christ if we are not also committed to a particular family of believers where the truth of our adoption into Christ is a lived reality with a specific group of people. We tend to approach our church families with a largely individualistic consideration: "What is in it for my benefit?" "Do I like it?" "Was it entertaining?" These questions are utter nonsense if we have a view of the church as a family.

For many people, their own identity as sons and daughters remains underdeveloped because they have not been committed to a local church. When we learn to walk in community, we discover that we are loved regardless of our performance and are forgiven, even in our sin. God's love for us finds a distinct expression in the form of a local church, and it is a grievous thing that many people have not experienced it! In our discipleship, it is essential that as we lead others to be secure in Christ, we involve them in our local church family. Discipleship is designed to function in the context of the church.

> There is no place in the Christian community for the serial monogamy concept where each new friendship comes with a shelf-life. When a relationship gets awkward, we do not simply move on to another connection. Instead, we dare to go on a life-long journey together through conflict and disappointment as well as seasons of mutual fascination and fun.... Our friendships survive seasons of vulnerability when people see our sin and somehow still choose our company.[17]
> — Pete Grieg

Lastly, our discipleship and evangelistic efficacy are directly connected to the degree of our security in the family. As Jesus himself said, it is our love for one another that demonstrates that we have received the love of Christ (John 13:35). The breaking down of racial, gender, age and socio-economic barriers is one of the primary works of the Holy Spirit and has been a part of nearly every major evangelistic movement in the last two millennia.

Respond

Have you tended to view the messiness of church as a reason to disengage or as an opportunity to press into relationships and see Jesus glorified?

Is the way you are living in community with your church leading to people around you asking about who Jesus is? What could you change to see that happen?

Living as a Church Family

From a discipleship standpoint, there are a few practical applications of church as family.

Hebrews 10:24-25

And let us watch out for one another to provoke love and good works, not neglecting to gather together, as some are in the habit of doing, but encouraging each other

First, we must be committed to building our lives so they are integrated with one another. It can be easy to give intellectual assent to this idea, but practically, rather than building our individual lives, we must ask the question of how we can invest in and build up the church family as a whole. The commitment to the church runs far deeper than a commitment to attend a service. It is a commitment to walk alongside one another in the complex, messy and difficult moments of our lives. This means that we journey alongside those we normally would never associate with — as family. We must open our homes and our hearts to our brothers and sisters as family, not merely as friends. We must be ready to sacrifice comfort and privacy for the sake of our family.

Second, we must earnestly desire to have others adopted into our family as a son or daughter of Christ and pray that Jesus breaks our heart for the lost in the same way that his own heart breaks. Paul talks about how this is a painful process (Galatians 4:19) — so painful that he analogizes it with childbirth. In this way, we put others ahead of ourselves. Our desire must be to see Christ formed in those around us: a desire that runs so deep it causes anguish when we fail to see it occur. When we forsake our preferences for the benefit of the whole, we are actually embodying Christ, who gave up the glories of Heaven for our benefit. Laying our lives down for our brothers and sisters is perhaps one of the most Jesus-like things we can do and, as such, is an essential component of being a son or daughter of Christ.

Hebrews 13:17

Obey your leaders and submit to them, since they keep watch over your souls as those who will give an account, so that they can do this with joy and not with grief, for that would be unprofitable for you.

Lastly, we must also invite others to refine us in our brokenness and sin. Our identity in Christ is forged when we submit ourselves to correction and rebuke from our leaders. We do not submit to one another as those who are already perfect. Instead, we submit to each other knowing that we all equally need the grace of Jesus! A church family is not built on our individual holiness, but rather on the fact that together, we are made holy by Jesus' holiness! We are not tolerant of sin; on the contrary, we deal with it seriously and directly. Crucially, our capacity to deal with sin in each other is predicated on a mutual commitment to the name of Jesus and his family: the church. We correct each other because we know that we love each other as brothers and sisters. Our correction is not a prerequisite to belong; rather, because we already belong, it is an invitation to live whole and full in Jesus' goodness!

Respond

Is there someone in your church family who you need to forgive? Have you been carrying any bitterness, hurt or frustration that you need to let go of?

Are you building your life alongside your brothers and sisters in the faith, or are you living for yourself? How might you change how you live so that you can encourage those around you to grow in their love of Jesus?

Summary

In this session, we discussed the importance of our identity as a son or daughter and a brother or sister in Christ. What a joy it is that we get to be part of the family of God! In particular:

- God planned from the beginning to adopt us as his children through Jesus — it wasn't an afterthought.
- We do not need to fear, for we have a good Father who longs to give us good gifts.
- Part of living as sons and daughters means that we must commit to a local church family.
- The way we treat our church family significantly affects our multiplication effectiveness.
- We must invite our brothers and sisters to help refine us.

Further Scripture Reading

If you would like to read more scripture on the topics in this session, please read:

- ☐ John 13:35
- ☐ Galatians 3:26
- ☐ James 3:14-18
- ☐ Ephesians 5:15-33
- ☐ Genesis 12

Questions for My Discipler

Write down a few questions that you would like to talk about with your discipler.

Discipleship Session 9

☐ **Prayer**

Spend time together in prayer, invite the Holy Spirit to guide your conversation. Take a moment to sit in silence as you prepare to listen to God's leading.

☐ **Celebration**

What can you celebrate since you last met? How is God moving in your lives? What discipleship stories can you share?

☐ **Review Previous Session**

Take a moment to review the previous session. Are there any discussion points or items that you need to follow up on?

☐ **Scripture**

Read two passages of scripture from the ones used in the session. Choose one that encouraged and one that challenged you.

☐ **God**

What are the primary attributes that you learned about God's character in this section? What encouraged or challenged you?

☐ **Yourself**

What did you learn about yourself from the above passages?

☐ Obedience

Does what you learned change the way you think?

Does what you learned about change the way you act?

Does what you learned about change the way you treat others?

☐ Questions

Take a moment to talk through the questions you had.

☐ Next Step

What is one step you can take between now and your next session to practice what you learned?

Who can you share what you learned with to help them know Jesus?

☐ Pray

Share concerns. Pray for one another. Invite the Holy Spirit to help you.

☐ Next Discipleship Session _____

10
Ambassadors & Slaves

This is the third session that will focus on secure identity: specifically, the missional identity of ambassador and the sacrificial identity of slave. Take a moment to thank Jesus for his invitation to a life of purpose before you begin.

Scripture Reading

To help you prepare, read the following scriptures on your own:

- ☐ 2 Corinthians 5:20
- ☐ John 17:17-20
- ☐ 1 Peter 2:11
- ☐ Matthew 20:26-28
- ☐ Romans 6:22

Respond

From the fairly intense language in the scripture above, write down your immediate reaction to the identities of ambassador and slave.

Ambassadors — Missional Identity

Jesus sent his disciples into the world as representatives of his Kingdom (John 17:18). His purpose in sending us into the world was so that others would hear about, and choose to accept, the message of Jesus (John 17:20). The apostle Paul recognized that the fact that we are sent into the world with a mission is not a task to complete but instead is an identity that we accept when we become followers of Jesus. The word that Paul uses is "ambassador," which means that we are sent as representatives of a kingdom; it is an identity statement, not a task statement.

2 Corinthians 5:20

We are ambassadors for Christ, since God is making his appeal through us. We plead on Christ's behalf: "Be reconciled to God."

The identity of an ambassador is one of great value and dignity. We have been invited to represent the Kingdom of God here on Earth! We, as ambassadors, are emissaries of the King of the Universe. A core part of Jesus' mission was to announce that the Kingdom of God had come. As Jesus himself demonstrated, the Kingdom of God is built on truth, grace, forgiveness and love. We, as recipients of his grace, are invited to represent that kingdom. This identity should give us great joy, confidence and security even in the face of great opposition. As ambassadors, we are secure no matter the situation in which we find ourselves, because we know that our King is sovereign on the throne.

> *Humanity's awesome dignity is found in its call to be the ambassador of God![18]*
> — Darrell Guder

There are two immediate and essential applications to seeing the identity of an ambassador take root. First, being an ambassador means that our allegiance is always to Jesus, never to this world. An ambassador can take up residence in a culture that is foreign to them, but they are never subsumed into that culture. No matter how long they reside in that culture, their primary responsibility will always be to the kingdom that has commissioned them as an ambassador.

Everything that an ambassador does in the foreign land is done in a manner that will strategically maximize their impact for the sending kingdom. Likewise, for us as ambassadors, it means that we must arrange our lives in such a way that our allegiance and priority is always to strategically maximize impact for the

Kingdom of Jesus. As ambassadors, we must resist the allure of success as defined by our culture. We must resist the false promises of comfort that are offered to us in our world and instead choose to do what is best for the Kingdom. The tension between our identity as an ambassador and the world around us will mean that we will often feel somewhat "alien" in our culture, as Peter states.

1 Peter 2:11 [NASB]

Beloved, I urge you as aliens and strangers to abstain from fleshly lusts which wage war against the soul.

The sense of being alien to our culture does not mean that we are weird or isolated; it means that we live according to a fundamentally different value set. We must continually resist the temptation to be absorbed into the culture around us. We should look radically different in how we structure our lives, spend our money, pursue our careers, serve our cities and love our families.

As ambassadors, our allegiance must always remain with Jesus; this is an inner-life aspect of our discipleship. However, the identity of an ambassador is about living strategically on mission so that people will hear about Jesus. The purpose of an ambassador is to represent the Kingdom, not passively, but actively. It means intentionally advocating for and introducing others to the way of Jesus. Paul's use of the word "plead" in the above verse in 2 Corinthians 5 is powerful. Pleading is an intentional, almost desperate, verb that indicates a sense of urgency and importance to the work. A fully formed identity as an ambassador should create a profound sense of urgency for us to see those around us know about Jesus. Multiplication is an inevitable product of the effective ambassador; we are inviting people into the Kingdom of Jesus and, in turn, sending them out as ambassadors in their own right.

A disciple who has a well-developed identity as an ambassador will show clear evidence of a life built upon a fundamentally different value system. Additionally, they will have a clear and demonstrated history of multiplication effectiveness stemming from their work.

Respond

Do you feel secure, despite sometimes being misunderstood or rejected, knowing that you represent a God who sits sovereign on the throne and a kingdom that is not of this world?

Do you feel the pressure to belong to our culture? How are you intentionally building daily and weekly rhythms to remind yourself that your first allegiance is to Jesus' Kingdom?

In what ways have you allowed the ideas of our culture to infiltrate your thinking? Perhaps ideas around relationships, sexuality, success, marriage, finances or happiness. What does Jesus teach?

How are you living into your identity as an ambassador as you plead with those around you to be reconciled to God?

Servants & Slaves — Sacrificial Identity

The crucial final identity marker that we are gifted is that of a slave or a servant. The identity of a servant or slave may be the most conceptually challenging of the identity statements. Jesus directly calls us to it in Matthew 20, and Paul reiterates this invitation in Romans 6.

Matthew 20:26-28

Instead, whoever wants to become great among you must be your servant, and whoever wants to be first must be your slave—just as the Son of Man did not come to be served, but to serve, and to give his life as a ransom for many.

Romans 6:22

But now, since you have been set free from sin and have become enslaved to God, you have your fruit, which results in sanctification—and the outcome is eternal life!

We serve others because we are called to become servants by the Gospel. The Gospel is news about how God became a man so that he could serve us. The creator God of the universe became the servant of his creation that had completely and utterly rejected him. We, in turn, are invited to live as servants ourselves. As Paul brilliantly points out in Romans 6, we are all ultimately enslaved to the things that we obey. In this sense, freedom is a myth; we are all playing the role of slave to the things that rule our lives. For many, this may be career, family, money, success, comfort or experiences. When we allow those things to enslave us, we are committing the sin of idolatry: permitting something other than God to take the primary place in our lives. For others, a direct habitual sin may be that which enslaves them. However, make no mistake, both the active sins and passive sins in our life that have our attention in place of Jesus are ultimately going to enslave us.

The fact that we are "slaves to the things we obey" is why understanding that we must be first enslaved to Christ is of paramount importance. To be enslaved to Christ is to establish him as the right, true and good Lord of our lives. To be his servant is to give him the rightly deserved authority to direct, steer and mould our lives. He has the power and the authority to give in great abundance or to take away as he wishes. Why is this such good news? It is good news because when we submit our lives to Jesus as Lord and adopt the posture of a servant, the process of sanctification begins to do the work of producing life within us (Romans

6:22). As we release the tight grip of control on our lives to him who is infinitely more capable, we can receive the fullness of life that he has to offer.

Respond

What are you currently enslaved to other than Christ (some common examples are social media, TV/Netflix, pornography, food, alcohol and so forth)? What could it look like for you to instead be enslaved to Christ?

How could you reallocate the energy used to serve yourself to instead serve and invest time in your relationship with Jesus?

Serving Others

Just as adopting the posture of a servant changes the way we relate to Jesus and build our lives, so too are our relationships transformed by this identity shift. Often when we serve, we can do so out of a sense of obligation or even a desire to see change happen in the world. However, there is a deeper motivation for serving others: identity. We do not serve simply because it is something good to do. We serve because we are a people who have adopted the identity of a servant. As our identity shifts to become that of a servant, serving becomes a natural extension of who we are; serving becomes our way of life.

Serving others can quickly feel like a task done in addition to the rest of our life. However, we are not called to serve others as an add-on to the lives that we live. We do not give "serving hours" or participate in "community service projects" in an effort to please Jesus. Such a compartmentalized understanding of serving does not flow from the identity of a servant; it is not deep enough and will only result in burnout. We are called to serve others because it is who we are. Every moment of every day, we are called to live into the posture and identity of a servant. The transformation of our identity into a servant means that we must build our lives to maximize our ability to serve and bless others, even ahead of our own need for comfort or ease.

Respond

How could you practically develop the habit of sacrificially serving others?

Do you view serving as a natural extension of who you are or a religious obligation?

How do you respond when you are not recognized by others for the ways in which you are serving?

Do you serve others only when it is convenient, practical or easy? When you get tired of serving do you seek to find "balance"? What did Jesus himself do in Matthew 20?

Summary

In this session, we discussed the importance of being an ambassador and a slave for Christ with the following key ideas:

- We are ambassadors for a good King, so our first allegiance is always to Jesus, not culture.

- We may feel somewhat alien in our culture, and that is okay.
- As ambassadors, we urgently seek to help people to know and live in relationship with God.
- We are all slaves to whatever we obey.
- We serve because it is who we are, not just what we do.
- Christian service is sacrificial in nature because we are modelled after Jesus.

Further Scripture Reading

If you would like to read more scripture on the topics in this session, please read:

- ☐ Philippians 3:20
- ☐ Colossians 3:1
- ☐ Philippians 2:1-11

Questions for My Discipler

Write down a few questions that you would like to talk about with your discipler.

Discipleship Session 10

☐ **Prayer**

Spend time together in prayer, invite the Holy Spirit to guide your conversation. Take a moment to sit in silence as you prepare to listen to God's leading.

☐ **Celebration**

What can you celebrate since you last met? How is God moving in your lives? What discipleship stories can you share?

☐ **Review Previous Session**

Take a moment to review the previous session. Are there any discussion points or items that you need to follow up on?

☐ **Scripture**

Read two passages of scripture from the ones used in the session. Choose one that encouraged and one that challenged you.

☐ **God**

What are the primary attributes that you learned about God's character in this section? What encouraged or challenged you?

☐ **Yourself**

What did you learn about yourself from the above passages?

☐ Obedience

Does what you learned change the way you think?

Does what you learned about change the way you act?

Does what you learned about change the way you treat others?

☐ Questions

Take a moment to talk through the questions you had.

☐ Next Step

What is one step you can take between now and your next session to practice what you learned?

Who can you share what you learned with to help them know Jesus?

☐ Pray

Share concerns. Pray for one another. Invite the Holy Spirit to help you.

☐ Next Discipleship Session _____

11

Identity Formation Through Suffering

Welcome to your 11th discipleship session. This is the final session that will focus on secure identity: specifically, how trials and suffering can help us develop our identity in Christ. Take a moment to praise Jesus for his faithfulness in your life.

Scripture Reading

To help you prepare, read the following scriptures on your own:

- ☐ Hebrews 12:1-11
- ☐ James 1:2-4
- ☐ Romans 5:1-5
- ☐ 2 Corinthians 10:9

Respond

Are there trials and challenges in your life that have helped you develop a greater faith in God? What are the current challenges you are facing that Jesus could use to help you trust him more?

Identity Formation Through Suffering

Many Christians know about their supposed identity in Christ. However, that identity is often a theoretical concept rather than a deeply rooted and formational belief. They know they ought to act, live and walk in confidence as sons and daughters; yet, for many, this does not describe their daily reality. When they run into challenges or doubt what is true about themselves, admonishing them with the Word can feel like piling shame on their unbelief. As disciple-making disciples, we work to create specific church families where we can learn to live as sons and daughters, servants and ambassadors by being brothers and sisters in Christ. How do we practically help people learn to walk out their identity, especially through the trials and valleys that life inevitably brings?

Scripture gives us a solution that is as shocking as it is counter-cultural. The authors of the New Testament describe a life of adversity, trials, suffering and discipline as the means by which we develop secure identities and robust Christ-like characters. These challenges that come up actually help us refine our identities as fully alive children, ambassadors and slaves.

> *Now I begin to be a disciple. Let fire and the cross; the crowds of wild beasts; let tearings, breaking and dislocations of bones; let cutting of members; let shatterings of the whole body; and let all the dreadful tortures of the devil come upon me; only let me get to Jesus Christ. All the pleasures of the world, and all the kingdoms of this earth, shall profit me nothing. It is better for me to die on behalf of Jesus Christ than to reign of all the ends of the earth.*[19]
> — Ignatius of Antioch

Discipline in Holiness

In Christ, we are set free from slavery to sin and raised from death to life. However, sin and brokenness still exist in us while we learn to yield to the sovereignty of Christ in us. Hebrews 12 teaches us that it is through discipline that our identity in Christ as sons and daughters is confirmed. By identifying sin and calling each other to repentance, we can simultaneously affirm dependence on Christ while urging each other to walk in our newfound freedom.

Hebrews 12:7-8,11

Endure hardship as discipline; God is treating you as his children. For what children are not disciplined by their father? If you are not disciplined—and everyone undergoes discipline—then you are not legitimate, not true sons and daughters at all. ... No discipline seems pleasant at the time, but painful. Later on, however, it produces a harvest of righteousness and peace for those who have been trained by it.

A life of continual and habitual sin will limit our formation as sons and daughters. Part of our mandate as disciple-making disciples is to call our brothers and sisters in Christ to radical holiness. The invitation to holiness can be painful as the private and shameful parts of our lives are brought into the light. As we confess our sins to one another and even suffer consequences associated with that sin, we are refined and established as more secure in Christ. We must teach people to be disciplined in righteousness. If we wish to disciple people towards security as sons and daughters, we must be willing to confront their sin and call them to wholeness in Christ. The pain caused by discipline is only temporary and is never done to earn acceptance by God. Discipline is a reminder that we are already loved and received in Christ, even though we still sin. Discipline and rebuke strengthen and remind us of our security in Christ.

Consequently, we must not tolerate actions or words that are not reflective of Christ in our midst, as they erode that identity. Our world flaunts and even brags about behaviour that is not honouring to Christ. Such flaunting of sin can include bragging about drunkenness, celebrating our gluttony, idolizing our possessions, tacitly endorsing violent and pornographic content, and sexual liberation. We must be disciplined in the pursuit of holy lives and be willing to be corrected when we miss the mark. When we call each other to a higher standard, we are reminding one another that we are sons and daughters of the King. Despite being painful, discipline and rebuke do not take away from our worth or security. Instead, they affirm it! That is why effective discipleship must involve both confronting the sin in those we are discipling and the humility to be challenged ourselves.

Respond

Do you feel shame connected to your sin? Did you know that you do not need to perform to be loved by God or by your church family? How do these truths change the way you live? Do you find freedom here?

Are there aspects of your life that you have been keeping hidden from others and God? Would you be willing to bring them into the light, even if there are consequences, knowing it will help you grow in Christ? Pray about this with your discipler.

Perseverance in Suffering

If discipline in righteousness affirms our identity as sons and daughters in Christ, then trials, challenges and adversity affirm our call to be servants and ambassadors. The culture around us teaches us that life is the most full, and we are the most alive, when everything is safe, secure and comfortable. There is nothing comfortable or safe about the call to be an ambassador or servant, apart from the security we have in Christ. We are conditioned to think that when something is uncomfortable, it means that something is wrong. Many of us, for good reason, fear being tired, poor, criticized or failing and so live lives that are safe and secure in the comforts afforded us by our Western society. The call to discipleship is the exact opposite; we give our lives for the benefit of others and the name of Jesus. This sacrificial way of living will surely involve trials and challenges, and as disciples, we will often feel tired and weak, but we need not despair or conclude that our lives are imbalanced.

James 1:2-4

Consider it pure joy, my brothers and sisters, whenever you face trials of many kinds, because you know that the testing of your faith produces perseverance. Let perseverance finish its work so that you may be mature and complete.

James teaches us that when we face all kinds of trials, we must consider it an opportunity to be made mature. We do not find the trial itself joy; instead, it is the knowledge that through the trial we will be brought into greater union with Christ that encourages us. Harmony with Christ is certainly cause for great joy! If a trial is the means and the end is Christ, then let us embrace the means with great eagerness. What a tremendously liberating theology when we look at adversity as conquerors, not victims. As those who have been sent on a mission for Jesus, we can thrive amid trials knowing that it will cause us to be more reliant and dependent on Jesus.

2 Corinthians 10:9

But he said to me, "My grace is sufficient for you, for my power is perfected in weakness."

For some, when they face trials, they despair and look for an easy way out. Others will double down on their efforts, grit their teeth and keep going. Both of these responses do not help forge a secure identity. Instead, we must allow the trial to strip away our fear of failure or discomfort, on the one hand, and self-reliance, on the other. We use adversity as an opportunity to cause us to look to Christ and depend on the power of the Holy Spirit.

Respond

Are you afraid of appearing weak or of actually being weak? Would you be willing to trust Jesus in your weaknesses so that he would be glorified? What might that look like?

Are you allowing a fear of failure, exhaustion or criticism to hold you back from fully stepping into your identity in Christ? Do you live boldly on mission for Jesus or do you allow fear to keep you from fully stepping into this call?

In what ways in your life are you pursuing comfort or running away from challenges because of fear? Might Jesus be calling you to trust him in those challenges?

Attitudes Towards Challenges

Romans 5:3-5

And not only that, but we also rejoice in our afflictions, because we know that affliction produces endurance, endurance produces proven character, and proven character produces hope. This hope will not disappoint us, because God's love has been poured out in our hearts through the Holy Spirit who was given to us.

It is very tempting to grumble, complain and fall into self-pity when things are challenging. We may be tempted to blame those around us for the challenges we are facing. When we take responsibility for the situation and choose an attitude of joy, our identity in Christ is strengthened. Trials, from a Biblical standpoint, are an opportunity for us to learn and deepen our security in Christ.

The call to be servants is, by its very definition, sacrificial and uncomfortable. There is nothing natural to our human pride about washing the feet of those around us, both metaphorically and literally as Jesus did in John 13. As we practice the uncomfortable habits of servanthood, our pride and self-reliance are stripped away. By serving others, we shift the attention away from ourselves and instead to the intrinsic value and worth of others. Few things will help strengthen our security in Christ quite like thinking about ourselves less.

To be formed in Christ amid the trial, we must surround ourselves with those who encourage us to persevere in the way of Jesus. We must not seek out the voices that advocate for the route that will produce comfort and security. We must surround ourselves with those who encourage us to continue faithfully in the mission set in front of us.

Perseverance should bear the fruit of hope within us. The more we persevere, the more we should be joyful and hopeful in our ministry. If we find ourselves becoming resentful or embittered, we must stop and turn to Jesus. If we find ourselves lacking in joy, then we are very likely attempting to serve in our own strength. In this regard, we are invited to be like Jesus, as described in Hebrews 12:2 — notice it was a joy for him to endure the cross?

Hebrews 12:1-2

Let us run with endurance the race that lies before us, keeping our eyes on Jesus, the source and perfecter of our faith. For the joy that lay before him, he endured the cross, despising the shame, and sat down at the right hand of the throne of God.

Lastly, the call to discipline and perseverance is ultimately a work of the Holy Spirit. If we seek to live as good disciple-making disciples in our own strength, we will be crushed into exhaustion or failure. We must continually invite the Holy Spirit to help us in our service.

Respond

Have you been complaining/grumbling about the challenges in your life? How could you replace it with a perspective of joyfully moving towards maturity and growth? Invite your discipler to share their perspective with you.

Do you have people around you who encourage you to persevere and have a positive attitude when things get tough? Do you lean on them during these trials, or do you withdraw and try to go in on your own strength?

Is there someone in your life who you can encourage to be faithful to serving in Jesus in a difficult season? Spend some time with them in prayer that Jesus would strengthen them.

Summary

God is able to use discipline, suffering and weakness to grow our trust and faith in him through the following ways:

- Discipline and transparency in our sin is necessary to see us grow in holiness and move towards Christ.
- We submit to discipline, knowing that we are loved in the church and by God.
- Suffering can be an opportunity to stretch our faith.
- As Christians, we endure challenges and do not give up easily, because our strength comes from Jesus, not ourselves.
- We carefully watch our attitudes and words when things are hard in order to be people of praise.

Further Scripture Reading

If you would like to read more scripture on the topics in this session, please read:

- ☐ Philippians 3:20
- ☐ Colossians 3:1
- ☐ Philippians 2:1-11

Questions for My Discipler

Write down a few questions that you would like to talk about with your discipler.

Discipleship Session 11

☐ **Prayer**

Spend time together in prayer, invite the Holy Spirit to guide your conversation. Take a moment to sit in silence as you prepare to listen to God's leading.

☐ **Celebration**

What can you celebrate since you last met? How is God moving in your lives? What discipleship stories can you share?

☐ **Review Previous Session**

Take a moment to review the previous session. Are there any discussion points or items that you need to follow up on?

☐ **Scripture**

Read two passages of scripture from the ones used in the session. Choose one that encouraged and one that challenged you.

☐ **God**

What are the primary attributes that you learned about God's character in this section? What encouraged or challenged you?

☐ **Yourself**

What did you learn about yourself from the above passages?

☐ Obedience

Does what you learned change the way you think?

Does what you learned about change the way you act?

Does what you learned about change the way you treat others?

☐ Questions

Take a moment to talk through the questions you had.

☐ Next Step

What is one step you can take between now and your next session to practice what you learned?

Who can you share what you learned with to help them know Jesus?

☐ Pray

Share concerns. Pray for one another. Invite the Holy Spirit to help you.

☐ Next Discipleship Session _____

Part 3

Missional Living

12
Simplicity & Integration

Welcome to your 12th discipleship session. This is the first session that will focus on missional living. We will talk about how simplicity and integration are two important keys to structuring our lives for Kingdom impact. Take a moment to pray for people in your life that you can help to know Jesus.

Scripture Reading

To help you prepare, read the following scriptures on your own:

- ☐ Philippians 4:11-13
- ☐ Ecclesiastes 12:12-13
- ☐ 2 Corinthians 11:28
- ☐ Matthew 6:33-34

Respond

Has God called you to be a missionary? Why or why not? Make a list below.

Missional Living

Missional living is the third discipleship emphasis and is the component of discipleship where we intentionally and strategically build our lives to maximize Kingdom impact.

Missional living is all about mission, but not our individual goals or dreams. Instead, it is about the great mission that Jesus has sent us on to see all people profess him as Lord. We are commanded to "go and make disciples." Missional living is about how we build lives that are effective in fulfilling this mission through intentional discipleship relationships.

Every follower of Jesus is called to be a missionary. To be a missionary is not a special call reserved for the spiritually elite. We are all missionaries for the Gospel; the only questions we need to be asking are where and how we should be maximizing our missional impact. The power of the Gospel is that it transforms every person into an agent of missional impact for the glory of Jesus. The Gospel is not just news about our spiritual transformation in Christ; it is equally an invitation for us to live a life of mission so that others can be made alive in Jesus.

We must ask, then, what does a missional life look like? How is it shaped and structured? How do we maximize our Kingdom impact? All of which are ultimately answered in the question: how do we live with Jesus as Lord?

As our Lord, Jesus has the authority to command every component of our lives. There is no part of who we are or what we are doing that is beyond his reach or separated from his command. His Lordship includes our work, family, relationships, jobs, finances, where and how we live, and what sorts of goals we set for our lives. The Apostle Paul proudly illustrates the power of a healthy missional life as he describes his attitude towards his own life, which notably included a great deal of hardship and suffering:

Philippians 4:11-13

I have learned to be content in whatever circumstances I find myself. I know both how to make do with little, and I know how to make do with a lot. In any and all circumstances I have learned the secret of being content—whether well fed or hungry, whether in abundance or in need. I am able to do all things through him who strengthens me.

His capacity to live a life of effective mission, especially when it was challenging, was directly connected to his surrendered and submitted posture towards Jesus (verse 13).

The surrender of our lives to Jesus leads us to an important principle of missional living: a missional life is not just effective for seeing people know Jesus, but it also leads to us being satisfied and fulfilled in Jesus. To live missionally does not mean that we form a specific vision for our lives; instead, it means we adopt Jesus' vision for our lives. As Paul says, *"For you died, and your life is now hidden with Christ in God"* (Colossians 3:1-4).

Jesus instructs us unambiguously to seek first his Kingdom above everything else. His Kingdom must come before any other desire, hope or dream. For many people, missional living is viewed as another way of religious thinking that can be added to their lives, but in actuality, it must be the entire framework which our life is built on.

Matthew 6:33-34

But seek first the kingdom of God and his righteousness, and all these things will be provided for you. Therefore don't worry about tomorrow, because tomorrow will worry about itself. Each day has enough trouble of its own.

Many of us fall into the temptation of putting career, security or comfort first with the good intentions to think missionally once our life is arranged to our liking. This kind of delayed missionality will never produce a genuinely missional life. A missional life will always desire the Kingdom of God first, above all else. We must first seek to glorify God in our lives, and only when the Kingdom of God is the deepest yearning and longing of our soul are we liberated from the idolatrous pursuit of our self-interest.

Jesus' commands to live a missional life are framed in broader teachings on worry and anxiety. The call to sacrifice, openness, passion and vulnerability are all grounded in our own security in Christ. From this understanding of our security in Christ and a desire to see him glorified, we can put the Kingdom before our doubts, fears and worries (Matthew 6:34). When we allow ourselves to place personal security, career, finances, fears, doubts and worries ahead of the Kingdom of God, with the noble notion that we want them to be satisfied with their lives, we are actually being ensnared by the lies of our culture. A missional life is a truly free life because it is a life with Jesus at the centre!

Respond

Do you view mission as something to do "in addition" to your life or as a part of everything you do?

Would you say that you are "seeking the kingdom first" in every area of your life? In what ways? Ask your discipler for their perspective.

Simplicity

There are two keys that work together to unlock a missional life: integration and simplicity.

Our lives are encumbered with all sorts of busy activities and commitments. Chasing success, accompanied by increasingly complex and expensive lives, is the norm in the Western world. Does our ferocious appetite for more actually add anything meaningful to our lives? Certainly not! Do our busy lives lead to contentment, much less missionality? Absolutely not!

The writer of Ecclesiastes thousands of years ago recognized the futility of our human busyness and striving. He invites us to lead simple lives of faithfulness and focus on the things of God.

Ecclesiastes 12:12-13

Of making many books there is no end, and much study wearies the body. Now all has been heard; here is the conclusion of the matter: Fear God and keep his commandments, for this is the duty of all mankind.

It is so easy to get distracted with all the opportunities in the world around us. Many of them are even good and beautiful! How do we decide what to do? Through the prophet Micah, God invites us to live lives of justice, faithfulness and humility (Micah 6:8). We need to live unencumbered, simple, honest and focused lives in order to faithfully walk out the call to be a disciple-making disciple.

Creators, Not Consumers

If we look at much of our busyness, we will discover that we spend a great deal of our time consuming. Moments spent consuming are the antithesis of simplicity. By definition, consumption means more and simplicity means less! A missional life will challenge our busyness and consumption. We cannot form the deep kind of relationships that discipleship requires if we are always busy pursuing our own interests or feeding ourselves. We must slow down and both intentionally and sacrificially create room for the non-believer to know the believer.

The missional life will consist of significant time, energy, resources and effort invested into the things of God. It is a full life, but not a busy life. A busy life is filled with activities, responsibilities, hobbies and interests that are all competing for attention. We all have 24 hours to invest each day, and each person spends all 24 of those hours every day. A busy life scatters those hours over a plethora of activities, many of which, if we are honest with ourselves, are self-serving. In a full life, we view those hours as a gift to be strategically invested. We may invest long hours and be tired or even exhausted at times as the Apostle Paul was (2 Corinthians 11:28). However, the investment is intentional and strategic rather than frantic and scattered.

2 Corinthians 11:28

I have laboured and toiled and have often gone without sleep; I have known hunger and thirst and have often gone without food; I have been cold and naked. Besides everything else, I face daily the pressure of my concern for all the churches.

The call to simplicity can be formed in us as disciples through two questions. First, we must ask, in what specific and measurable way will this decision increase our missional effectiveness? We must be honest with ourselves in this regard. The human heart can rationalize all kinds of things that are not of the heart of God. It is easy to justify an increased standard of living or the need to carve out large amounts of leisure time. We live in a culture that idolizes vacations and "me time" under the guise of necessity. This is not to say that rest is inherently bad; however, so often it is the goal above all else. Further, when it really comes down to it, often we are not prioritizing rest in these moments, but consumption. In the missional life, we seek first the Kingdom of God instead of chasing our momentary desires.

Second, we must ask, what are the potential negative missional consequences of this decision? For example, we may get a job that could legitimately open up new missional opportunities, but if it pulls us out of our discipleship relationships and church family, then that is a very dangerous situation. We must stop and seriously reflect on our motivations for our decision making and the consequences associated with them.

Respond

Do you think, perhaps subconsciously, that more stuff or better experiences will lead to a happier life? How could you shift your thinking to be more in line with a missional view like Paul's in Philippians 4?

What major decisions (relationship, job, place to live, choice of school program) have you intentionally made for the purpose of seeing people know Jesus? What decisions are you facing in the future that you can think about in a missional way?

What is something you can stop doing in your life that will create more simplicity and allow for greater missionality?

Integration

The second key is integration. Often when we think of our lives, we tend to isolate the different components from one another. In many cases, we may even seek to prevent the elements of our lives from touching one another.

An example of this compartmentalization is the popular phrase "work-life balance." While the intention of healthy, sustainable lives is commendable, the concept is dangerous. Work and life are not opposing forces or segments of our lives. When living missionally, instead of seeking to maximize "work-life balance," we seek to maximize "Kingdom impact." The goal is to take all of the components of our lives and see them integrated to be an effective Gospel witness.

In a compartmentalized view of our lives, the Gospel, church and the mission of our lives are all merely single compartments. As a particular compartment grows, it will naturally squeeze out some of the other compartments, as illustrated below. In a compartmentalized view of our lives, the Gospel/church are always competing for attention.

Such compartmentalization can, if not corrected, result in resentment towards the church, as we feel torn between serving the church and caring for ourselves. Given enough time, this can ultimately lead to a life that is self-centred as we relegate the mission of God to the back-burner or let it become forgotten altogether. We are the most alive when we are committed to the mission of God; this call, however, will not always be easy.

If compartmentalization is the opposite of missional living, then what is the alternative? The answer lies in living an integrated life

A Non-Missional Life - No Integration

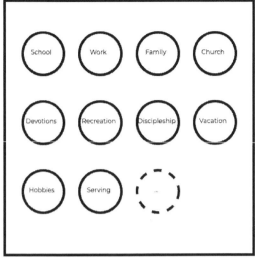

A non-missional life avoids integration. Lacks purpose and intentionality to maximize kingdom impact.

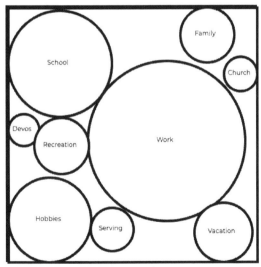

As things get "busy" discipleship/church relationships get squeezed out.

where every component of our lives seeks to facilitate the common goal of maximizing Kingdom impact. If we intentionally arrange every part of our lives such that they are all pointing towards the same goal, then instead of one area competing with another, they will all work together to facilitate the same purpose. Instead of "work and life" being opposing forces, our work, rest and play will all be leveraged to see people know Jesus.

James 4:13-17 addresses the temptation to compartmentalize our lives such that our missional impact is ignored. Instead of compartmentalizing, which he calls evil, we are instructed to ask the question, *"What is the heart of God?"*

James 4:13-17

Come now, you who say, "Today or tomorrow we will travel to such and such a city and spend a year there and do business and make a profit." Yet you do not know what tomorrow will bring — what your life will be! For you are like vapour that appears for a little while, then vanishes. Instead, you should say, "If the Lord wills, we will live and do this or that." But as it is, you boast in your arrogance. All such boasting is evil. So it is sin to know the good and yet not do it.

James calls us to pause our lives and seek to know the purposes of God in our lives. We can make plans that may be fruitful in the eyes of the world. We may be able to accomplish a great deal, but in the perspective of eternity, our plans do not amount to much. James is instructing us to live integrated lives that align with God's heart for the nations instead of compartmentalized ones.

River of Integration

A helpful illustration for understanding what an integrated life for mission looks like is that of a large river with several tributaries that are flowing into it. The central river of our lives exists to carry the Gospel. The tributaries are the various parts of our lives, all providing fuel for the movement of the Gospel. When we live missionally, every component of our lives is serving the same goal: Jesus' glory through the movement of the Gospel!

When we are not living missionally, the tributaries are cut off from the main river and result in standing and stagnant water. Stagnant water eventually grows scum and fails to support life.

A Missional Life - Integration

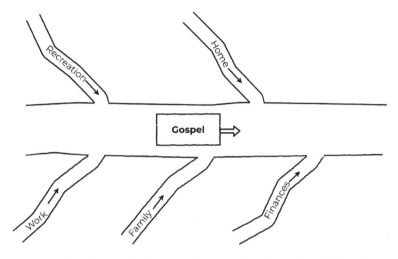

Tributaries contributing to an integrated life that carries the Gospel.

Respond

Do you try to separate your Christian and non-Christian friends? How might you naturally start to introduce them to each other?

Draw your own 'missional river.' What parts of your life are not connected to the mission of introducing people to Jesus?

Have you made big plans for your future? How do those plans help you lead people to Jesus and glorify God?

What decisions do you have to make right now? How can you make these decisions in light of living a missional life?

Summary

A missional life is all about structuring our lives so that people will know Jesus. We do this in a number of ways:

- We start by surrendering to Jesus as Lord of every area of our lives.
- Missional living can be challenging, but Jesus promises to support us and give us the strength and joy to serve him.
- Simplicity is important; we do less so that we can intentionally invest in the Kingdom.
- Missional living involves integrating rather than compartmentalizing our faith.
- We need to intentionally make plans that centre on the heart of God rather than our individual success.

Further Scripture Reading

If you would like to read more scripture on the topics in this session, please read:

- ☐ Micah 6:8
- ☐ James 4:13-17
- ☐ Psalm 73
- ☐ John 7:38
- ☐ Colossians 3:1-4

Questions for My Discipler

Write down a few questions that you would like to talk about with your discipler.

Discipleship Session 12

☐ **Prayer**

Spend time together in prayer, invite the Holy Spirit to guide your conversation. Take a moment to sit in silence as you prepare to listen to God's leading.

☐ **Celebration**

What can you celebrate since you last met? How is God moving in your lives? What discipleship stories can you share?

☐ **Review Previous Session**

Take a moment to review the previous session. Are there any discussion points or items that you need to follow up on?

☐ **Scripture**

Read two passages of scripture from the ones used in the session. Choose one that encouraged and one that challenged you.

☐ **God**

What are the primary attributes that you learned about God's character in this section? What encouraged or challenged you?

☐ **Yourself**

What did you learn about yourself from the above passages?

☐ Obedience

Does what you learned change the way you think?

Does what you learned about change the way you act?

Does what you learned about change the way you treat others?

☐ Questions

Take a moment to talk through the questions you had.

☐ Next Step

What is one step you can take between now and your next session to practice what you learned?

Who can you share what you learned with to help them know Jesus?

☐ Pray

Share concerns. Pray for one another. Invite the Holy Spirit to help you.

☐ Next Discipleship Session _____

13

The Acts 2 Church & Everyday Practices

Welcome to your 13th discipleship session. This is the first of three sessions that will develop missional living by looking at the early church in Acts and developing everyday practices from them. Take a moment to dream about what kind of church you would like to be a part of.

Scripture Reading

To help you prepare, read the following scriptures on your own:

- [ ] Acts 2:42-47
- [ ] Matthew 6:6-13, Acts 4:42
- [ ] 1 Peter 2:9
- [ ] Revelation 1:5-6

Respond

What kind of church family do you want to be a part of? How does it line up with what you read in Acts 2?

Everyday Practices

Having laid the groundwork with the importance of living an integrated life for missional impact, we must ask the question: what does it look like in practice? A great case study in what missional living looks like is found in Acts 2, shortly after the birth of the church. From it, we have identified six everyday practices that marked the missional church.

Acts 2:42-47

They devoted themselves to the apostles' teaching, to the fellowship, to the breaking of bread, and to prayer. Everyone was filled with awe, and many wonders and signs were being performed through the apostles. Now all the believers were together and held all things in common. They sold their possessions and property and distributed the proceeds to all, as any had need. Every day they devoted themselves to meeting together in the temple, and broke bread from house to house. They ate their food with joyful and sincere hearts, praising God and enjoying the favour of all the people. Every day the Lord added to their number those who were being saved.

Everyday Practice 1: Spiritual Hunger

There will be a lot of discussion on fellowship and breaking bread. However, before we can discuss those, we need to emphasize the necessity of spiritual hunger as exemplified in the devotion to the apostles' teaching and prayer.

Spiritual hunger is the fuel that drives our missional lives. As we feed our appetite for more of God, we, in turn, begin to live missionally, which, in turn, causes us to be more spiritually hungry. Spiritual hunger is all about dependence on the Lord. When we live on mission, we live as people who daily turn to the Lord in total and complete surrender. We surrender to be moulded by God, to be sanctified and to invite the Lord to send us on mission through multiplication.

If Christians do not energetically awaken and if God does not pour out His Spirit, the world will laugh at the church.[20]
— Charles Finney

Prayer

A missional life, by definition, is a life of bold faith. The church in Acts was utterly dependent on the work of the Holy Spirit in their midst. A missional church is ultimately sustained and supported by the work of God. We cannot live missionally without reliance on God's grace and power. When we live missionally, we should be living with the faith that God will move in our midst and do what we cannot do.

Prayer is a deeply missional activity. Any missional work that does not come from the place of prayer is almost certainly tainted with our pride and sin. It is to help resist the temptation to operate out of our pride that Jesus instructed us to pray that the Lord's kingdom would come, that the Lord's will would be done, that what we see on earth would align with His purposes. Jesus instructed us to pray for the mission (Matthew 6:10)! It is through daily surrender before the Lord in prayer that the Lord's desires become ours.

> *When a vision is born in the pride of a prayer-less imagination, it is nothing more than a projection of the self. Self-projected vision is beamed indiscriminately onto the world by an inner drive to be larger than life in every conversation, in every context and in posterity too. Self-projected vision is an empire building compulsion; it comes not to serve but to be served.*[21]
> — Pete Grieg

Matthew 6:9-10

Therefore, you should pray like this: Our Father in heaven, your name be honored as holy. Your kingdom come. Your will be done on earth as it is in heaven.

This act of surrendering is a daily recurring rhythm. When we take a step of faith to live on mission, we will often begin in a place of prayer but then will begin to run on our own strength, hoping in vain that our spiritual high from months or years ago will carry us. Spiritual hunger and prayer must be a daily practice that occurs both in private (Matthew 6:6) and in the community (Acts 4:24).

In a missional life, we daily bring the needs, hopes and dreams of the entire discipleship movement before the Lord. Out of a place of awareness of our dependence on God, we are sent on mission. The pattern that we see in Acts is very clear: the disciples prayed, experienced God and were sent on mission. A missional life, empowered by the Holy Spirit, starts with prayer!

Respond

How often do you pray for the Lord to give you a heart for mission? How often do you pray for the mission of your church?

What is one way you could incorporate prayer with others into your weekly or daily schedule?

Submitting to Teaching

With the foundation laid in prayer, a key part of healthy spiritual hunger is a willingness to be corrected by the teaching of the church. With the apostles leading the way, the church began to put into action what they were being taught. Their willingness to actually live what they were taught meant that the church had the humility to change how they were thinking to reflect Jesus better.

Missional living requires that we are submitted to the broader community and willing to allow God to use the church, particularly the leadership, to challenge our thinking and living. Again, this is a countercultural principle. We are typically conditioned to think very autonomously or individualistically. In a missional life, we learn to think communally and submit to one another.

This spiritual hunger and willingness to grow and learn are always coupled to a supernatural move of God. A missional life is a supernatural life. A desire for the supernatural is never for our benefit or pride. Rather, we must desire the move of God so that church family will be strengthened and non-believers will proclaim God's goodness. (1 Corinthians 14:12,25)

1 Corinthians 14:12

So also you—since you are zealous for spiritual gifts, seek to excel in building up the church.

In this way, boldness to invite people to know Jesus must always be the overflow of a fervent, passionate, desperate and faithful public and private prayer life and time in the word.

Discipling Spiritual Hunger

Spiritual hunger is not something that you are born with or not; neither is it something that you have or not. Rather, spiritual hunger is something that we develop. Spiritual hunger is not cultivated by consuming more sermons, finding a better preacher or engaging in trendy worship. When we approach those things as if they exist for ourselves, we only fuel and satisfy our own narcissism. Spiritual hunger requires that we come to Jesus in humility, asking him to mould our hearts. We cultivate spiritual hunger by asking the Lord to soften our hearts so that we can clearly hear his voice. A soft heart is marked by one who can identify, by the work of the Holy Spirit, their sinful desires and pride, and ask the Lord to give them new desires and longings.

Spiritual hunger is cultivated by coming before the Lord in prayer and submitting to the power of his word: both in our times of quiet on our own as well as through collective times with our missional family — the church. The church cultivates spiritual hunger in a two-fold process. First, the church calls people to a process of knowing and being transformed by Jesus — sanctification through prayer and the word. Second, the mandate of the church is to missionally mobilize people who have encountered Jesus. Spiritual hunger without a missional edge is not true spiritual hunger. Spiritually hungry people will yearn to be sent on mission so that others will know Jesus. In short, spiritual hunger and multiplication go hand in hand.

Respond

When you listen to sermons or preaching are you primarily looking for information that will help you be a better person, or are you looking to be more in love with Jesus? How do you know?

How could you encourage others around you to develop spiritual hunger?

How will you continue to cultivate a spiritual hunger in yourself? Is this something that you are struggling with right now?

Everyday Practice 2: Church at the Centre

42 They devoted themselves to the apostles' teaching, to the fellowship, to the breaking of bread, and to prayer...
46 Every day they devoted themselves to meeting together in the temple, and broke bread from house to house.

The first component of the early church's integrated life is that the church was at the centre of how they lived their lives. Missional living is always in the context of community. We cannot live missionally on our own. We are not lone-rangers or islands unto ourselves. Rather, we are invited to be committed to the body of Christ in the context of a local church. However, this goes far deeper than a mere once-a-week commitment. The church integrated their lives such that they were in constant contact with both one another and unbelievers. Church not a once a week "event" that they attended; instead, it was a family of believers who were on a mission together 24/7. Let us state clearly: to live missionally is to change our thinking about church from an event or building to a family committed to one another with our whole lives.

To the early believers, the church was their family. They were devoted to one another. They were committed to one another through thick and thin, even at significant personal cost. The church was not a relationship of convenience but one of mutual investments into one another and commitment to the cause of Christ. The commitment to one another as the body of Christ is what it means to be a covenant family. We are not family by our own blood; we are family by the blood of Christ who has invited us into a new family (1 Peter 2:9, Revelation 1:5-6).

Revelation 1:5-6

To him who loves us and has set us free from our sins by his blood, and made us a kingdom, priests to his God and Father

We have limited relational capacity in our lives. There are only so many people we can build meaningful relationships with at the same time. Discipleship relationships require significant time and energy invested in them, as do relationships with non-believers. By placing church at the centre of our lives, we seek to integrate all of our relationships into our church family relationships. By way of metaphor, our church family serves as the hub to which all the spokes of our relationships connect. Normally, we tend to silo or isolate our relationships from one another. Our work, school, church, family and hobby relationships may never interact! By placing church at the centre, we seek to bring all of our primary day-to-day relationships together in our church family. This does not mean that we avoid relationships with non-believers — quite the opposite! We seek instead to integrate our lives so that our non-christian friends have regular interactions with our brothers and sisters in Christ.

Placing church at the centre is risky, as we are opening our lives and ourselves up to the possibility of being hurt or wounded by those we are journeying with. Deep relationships and deep discipleship require the very real possibility of being hurt. To be truly known and truly loved, we must open our lives up to one another and build lives where the good, the bad and the ugly are all part of journeying towards Christ together.

Missional living with church at the centre is undoubtedly a fantastic context for a life of security in the context of community. However, how exactly is it missional? How does orienting our lives around church family increase missional impact?

1) People will know us by our love

John 13:35

By this everyone will know that you are my disciples, if you love one another.

Our witness in the context of church family is perhaps the most powerful witness that we have (John 13:35). When people see a missionally mobilized family of believers, it should be immediately apparent to those who look on from the outside. As Christians, our mission is to call people to be secure as sons and daughters in Christ. How much more effective is our witness when people can see that identity expressed in unity and harmony (Psalm 133:1)? As the world becomes more and more self-focused and isolated, living in vulnerability with a church community becomes more attractive to those looking in from the outside. A loving community built on more than similar interests, personalities or lifestyles, but instead formed through the Holy Spirit, is profoundly attractive to those who have no context for such a community.

2) Our witness of Jesus is collective rather than individual

When we seek to introduce people to Jesus by ourselves, our witness is always incomplete and flawed. We point people to Jesus, but we do that as flawed and imperfect representatives. If the only witness that people have in their lives is us, then we are only introducing them to a small dimension of who Jesus is. Of course, an individual witness is still fantastic, and we must celebrate it. However, when we witness as individuals alongside our brothers and sisters in the faith, our impact is that much stronger. By placing church at the centre, the entire community can serve as a witness. When we are broken or fail, we can demonstrate to those who do not know Jesus that even in our weaknesses and brokenness, Jesus is still good. As the family of Christ rallies, they help people see a bigger and fuller picture of who Jesus is.

3) The context for conversion is safe

For many people, the invitation to follow Jesus is profoundly risky. Such a risk is especially true for those from backgrounds and cultures where the Gospel is not prominent. Accepting Jesus may mean that they could be disowned, or worse, by their families (Mark 10:28-31). If we are going to see people know Jesus when there is such a risk, we must provide a family that will support, encourage, uphold and resource those brothers and sisters.

One important consideration when seeking to implement church at the centre is that we do not isolate ourselves in a bubble. The community itself must always be missional and oriented around that mission. We must remain vigilant and alert to the temptation to build insular communities where serious engagement with those who do not know Jesus is limited.

Respond

When people look at the way you interact with your church family, are they getting a clear picture of what Jesus is like? Why or why not?

Do you treat your participation in church as a weekly or multiple times a week event? Or do you see your church as your family? Why or why not?

How could you live in a way so that people feel more included in your church family, especially those who do not know Jesus?

How could you simply adjust your weekly schedule to involve your church family on a more natural and daily basis?

Identify some areas in the lives of those you are discipling where you can call them to greater missional living. Are they living lives that integrate believers and non-believers? Or do they tend to isolate the two groups?

Summary

The early church lived in a radical, beautiful and integrated missional community. We can learn a few important things from them.

- The starting place for missional living is cultivating a spiritual hunger.
- We develop spiritual hunger by spending time in prayer and in scripture.
- Spiritual hunger develops when we submit to one another in the church and ask for God to move in our midst.
- By placing church at the centre, we can integrate our relationships in a healthy way to see people know Jesus.

- Church is intended to operate as a family 24/7 instead of a weekly event.

Further Scripture Reading

If you would like to read more scripture on the topics in this session, please read:

- [ ] Psalm 133:1
- [ ] 1 Corinthians 14:12,25
- [ ] Mark 10:28-31

Questions for My Discipler

Write down a few questions that you would like to talk about with your discipler.

Discipleship Session 13

☐ **Prayer**

Spend time together in prayer, invite the Holy Spirit to guide your conversation. Take a moment to sit in silence as you prepare to listen to God's leading.

☐ **Celebration**

What can you celebrate since you last met? How is God moving in your lives? What discipleship stories can you share?

☐ **Review Previous Session**

Take a moment to review the previous session. Are there any discussion points or items that you need to follow up on?

☐ **Scripture**

Read two passages of scripture from the ones used in the session. Choose one that encouraged and one that challenged you.

☐ **God**

What are the primary attributes that you learned about God's character in this section? What encouraged or challenged you?

☐ **Yourself**

What did you learn about yourself from the above passages?

☐ Obedience

Does what you learned change the way you think?

Does what you learned about change the way you act?

Does what you learned about change the way you treat others?

☐ Questions

Take a moment to talk through the questions you had.

☐ Next Step

What is one step you can take between now and your next session to practice what you learned?

Who can you share what you learned with to help them know Jesus?

☐ Pray

Share concerns. Pray for one another. Invite the Holy Spirit to help you.

☐ Next Discipleship Session _____

14

Intentional Proximity & Open Home

Welcome to your 14th discipleship session. We will be looking at the everyday practices of intentional proximity and open home. As you begin, thank God for the people in your life who he has used to disciple you.

Scripture Reading

To help you prepare, read the following scriptures on your own:

- ☐ Acts 2:42-47
- ☐ 1 Thessalonians 2:7-8
- ☐ Hebrews 13:2
- ☐ John 1:1-14

Respond

Make a list below in response to these questions. How did you choose to live where you are living? What factors influenced who you are living with? Which of the factors were missional?

Everyday Practice 3: Intentional Proximity

When examining the book of Acts, it is clear to see that the early followers of Jesus were in intentional proximity with one another. Likewise, when living missionally, our work, home, play and church family must be all near one another.

44 Now all the believers were together and held all things in common.... Every day they devoted themselves to meeting together in the temple, and broke bread from house to house.

The above familial relationships with our church are not possible without being physically close to one another. Furthermore, it is exceedingly difficult to integrate our work or school relationships into the pursuit of Jesus if they are not close to us. The daily contact exhibited by the disciples was critical. So often, our lives are fragmented geographically with the various components of our lives all in different places. Effective integration of the 'tributaries' of our lives requires that we actually connect all the pieces. This is illustrated in the diagram below.

Intentional Proximity

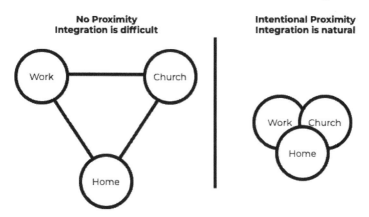

The requirement for proximity may be one of the more challenging components for missional living in 21st century Western culture, where lengthy commutes to work or play are the norm. However, at a bare minimum, our church family and our living should be as close together as possible, ideally within walking distance of one another to maximize integration.

John 1:14 [MSG]

The Word became flesh and blood, and moved into the neighbor-hood.

We must desire to be like Jesus, who moved into our neighbour-hood, so that we could be saved; so, we move into neighbour-hoods with the same missional desire.

Intentionality

Intentional proximity means that we choose, deliberately, for integration and missional living to be the crucial driving factors in deciding where and how we live. The default cultural norm is to put either our biological family or our career first as our primary driving factors; intentional proximity instead places missional efficacy first as the primary factor.

Many disciples have good intentions for living missionally, but slowly over time, the temptation for upwards mobility, purchasing a house, getting a better house or prioritizing our career causes us to compromise where we live and, thus, compromise missionality.

In many cases, a person will get a job and immediately move because of the apparent logistical implications. We will often minimize our commute to work but increase our commute to our core relationships and missional church family. Why do we accept that in the church world? In missional living, glorifying Jesus and seeing people know him through our witness as Gospel proclaimers must be the motivating factor in our lives.

We must resist the cultural pressure to choose career, comfort, luxury, trendiness or other worldly desires as determining factors for where we live. Instead, we must choose to value proximity with the people we love and the mission we are called to more highly. We must not trade relationships for the things of this world or treat church, discipleship and closeness as if they are dispensable or easily replaceable.

Healthier Rhythms & Spontaneity

One significant benefit of intentional proximity is that it enables a far more sustainable and healthy rhythm for discipleship. Intentional proximity minimizes commuting time, maximizes relational time and creates avenues for spontaneity in our relationships. Paul highlights this brilliantly in 1 Thessalonians.

1 Thessalonians 2:7-8

Just as a nursing mother cares for her children, so we cared for you. Because we loved you so much, we were delighted to share with you not only the gospel of God but our lives as well.

Paul lived so that those he was discipling had direct, local access to his life. When he was starting churches, he intentionally lived so that people would have access to him. He uses the compelling picture of a nursing mother to indicate the kind of close, dependent, ongoing and immediate access that discipleship and missional relationships require. As with a nursing mother, intentional proximity is essential for the health of the disciple and the discipler. Similarly, deliberate proximity creates opportunities for spontaneity in our relationships. We cannot form the kind of deep relationships that missional living requires if our relationships are always scheduled. Spontaneity, enabled by being close to one another, allows us to see people as they really are.

Sharing proximity with one another is why communal living is a natural byproduct of missional living. If we are living missionally, then we will see dense pockets of community form around that mission.

Respond

Are you connecting with those you are in a discipleship relationship with often enough to see the "real" version of who they are?

Would you be willing to move your house so that you could be close to those in the church? Are we willing to call those we are discipling to do likewise?

Do you treat your church relationships like they are easily replaceable? Are relationships more important than career or comfort? Why or why not?

Where might Jesus be calling you to live so that you can lead others to know him?

Have you allowed worldly desires such as a nicer apartment or neighbourhood to decide where you live instead of where you would have the biggest impact for Jesus? What could you do differently?

Everyday Practice 4: Open Home

> 46 Every day they devoted themselves to meeting together in the temple, and broke bread from house to house.

Twice in Acts 2:42-47 it mentions that they "broke bread" (shared meals) together. The most mundane and yet profoundly impactful way to integrate our lives is the sharing of meals and the opening of our homes. In our culture, the home acts as a private refuge for a personal retreat; it is where we isolate ourselves from one another. However, in a missional life, the home becomes the gathering place for mission! The home is an essential tool of a missional life.

It can be used to gather people, teach the Gospel, lead people to Jesus, pray together, process hurt together and celebrate wins.

The mission was not an addition to the lives of the people in Acts; no, the mission was their life! Following their example, every component of our lives becomes a tool that we can use to serve the cause of Jesus. Living missionally transforms the simple, daily tasks that we tend to see as irrelevant into tools used for Jesus' glory. Our possessions and homes, indeed our entire lives, do not belong to us. Yet for many disciples, there is a line that we have drawn, often around our homes, where Christ does not have total dominion and discipleship is excluded. A home may be a place for private spiritual refuge, but what if we were to view it from the perspective of multiplying discipleship and missional living?

Open Lives

All of our lives must be part of the mission to raise and send disciple-making disciples. Open homes (or dorms and apartments) are part of open lives. As disciple-makers, we must live with openness and vulnerability, allowing people to see our strengths as well as our weaknesses. An active Christian witness must include the ability for people to see who we really are, not just a refined projection of an idealistic Christ follower. When we invite people into our lives, especially the raw and messy parts, we are allowing them to see how the power of Jesus' grace works.

> *Radically ordinary hospitality begins when we remember that God uses us as living epistles and that the openness or inaccessibility of our homes and hearts stands between life and death, victory and defeat, and grace or shame for most people.*[22]
> — **Rosaria Butterfield**

One of Jesus' disciples, Simon, invited Jesus to heal his sick mother-in-law in her home. After a day of long ministry, late in the day, Jesus headed to her home and miraculously healed her. Immediately after being healed by Jesus, Simon's mother-in-law began to serve Jesus and open her home up for the entire town to encounter Jesus (Mark 1:29-31). She took her home, her place of refuge, and because of Jesus' grace, transformed it into a refuge for others. Our homes are not our private castles where we hoard our treasures, but sanctuaries to which we welcome with open arms those who need to encounter the death-to-life transformation available to them in Jesus.

Each of us has people who we can uniquely reach and welcome into our lives. There are those whom no one else can reach other than us. When we think about our lives from a missional standpoint, our homes, apartments, dorms and student houses are tools that we can use to become a place of refuge for those in our world to come and encounter Jesus in a real, tangible and practical way. Homes are raw, messy and authentic and, as a result, provide the perfect environment to expose people to the grace of Jesus — both those we are discipling and those who do not yet know Jesus. The home is perhaps one of the most natural ways to bring together those who know Jesus and those who do not.

Hospitality

Hospitality and opening our homes lie at the centre of an effectively integrated missional life. We eat meals many times a week; each of those is an opportunity to create community and live on mission by inviting people to join us at the table to share a meal. The liberating aspect of this is that an open home does not require a great deal of effort. We do not need to host to impress people; no, we invite people into our homes as part of the natural rhythm of our lives lived on mission. Practically, we are not just inviting others to our homes for specially prepared meals on our fancy china. Instead, we are inviting others into our messy homes for leftovers.

Open homes are about valuing and cherishing people. In many homes, the TV is at the centre of the house with the couches arranged to consume content. In an open home, we structure our homes around people to love. What if our homes were structured so that the couches faced each other? This suggestion is both metaphorical and literal. When building open homes, we trade our televisions for dinner tables. We arrange our couches so that we see each other's smiles and tears and break down the barriers that separate us. Addressing loneliness may be one of the oldest and deepest human needs.

> *Hospitality is necessary whether you have cat hair on the couch or not. People will die of chronic loneliness sooner than they will cat hair in the soup.*[23]
> — Rosaria Butterfield

Open Homes are Costly

Open homes and open lives are profoundly costly to our finances, schedules and pride. On a practical level, we open our lives up with generosity. An open home is not a tit-for-tat relationship. An open home is one where we give generously without expecting anything in return. On a practical level, it costs money to host people. Part of discipleship in missional living is learning to view that cost as a Kingdom investment that we are privileged to make.

Secondly, open homes are costly to our schedules. Appointments and schedules drive much of our lives. Of course, schedules and appointments are essential and necessary to create a sustainable routine; however, our lives can end up so over-scheduled that there is no room to provide the spontaneous and compassionate care that an open home requires. An open home means that we intentionally create time and space in our lives through which people can enter our lives. An open life means that we may have to sacrifice our preferred schedule, slow down and invest in someone in need. Discipleship is not always convenient or practical. The responsibility of a disciple-maker is to be willingly, eagerly and joyfully giving of themselves for others.

Lastly, an open home will cost us our pride. If we attempt to always be perfect and in control, we will either inevitably fail in that pursuit or exhaust ourselves in the process. An open home requires that we do not strive to impress or have everything in perfect order to uphold a false perception of who we are in others' minds.

Start Where You Are

The invitation to an open home can be intimidating and scary. We are discussing how the private, even intimate, moments of our lives are used for Jesus' glory. Instead of viewing this everyday practice as an insurmountable task, we should instead take it as an encouragement to start making small changes. We should start wherever we are and begin to take steps to intentionally and sacrificially open our lives up. The process will require some trial and error as we learn to open our lives and possessions up for the benefit of others. That's okay! Failure is not final in discipleship.

Every person's home situation is unique, and in some cases, the kind of openness described above may not be possible. We must ask how we can foster an open home environment wherever we are. We must find ways that it can work rather than looking at all the reasons it is disruptive and challenging.

Respond

Do you view your home or personal space as your own? How might you be more generous with it?

Is your life so busy that there is no space for spontaneous hospitality? How can you open up more space in your schedule to increase missional spontaneity?

Make a list of the barriers that you have toward being hospitable. Share them with your discipler, and try to work through them one at a time.

For how many meals a week could you intentionally invite people to join you?

Is your "private life" something that would lead others to Christ if they were invited to see it? Why or why not?

How can you invite those you are discipling to also open up their homes? Is this something that comes naturally to them or is it a challenge?

Summary

Missional living involves the very practical aspects of our lives, including where we live and how we use our homes or dorm rooms. We talked about how:

- Effective integration requires that we intentionally live near both the people we hope to reach and our church family.
- Intentional proximity allows us to live with healthier rhythms.
- We must resist worldly pressure to live in a nice house; instead, we must choose to live where we will have the greatest impact.
- Our homes, dorms and apartments are all tools the Lord has given us to reach and bless others.
- We need to simplify our lives so that we can create space to invite people into.

Further Scripture Reading

If you would like to read more scripture on the topics in this session, please read:

- ☐ Luke 19:1-10
- ☐ Luke 22:14
- ☐ Acts 2:1-4
- ☐ Mark 1:29-31

Additional Reading

Rosaria Butterfield's book, *The Gospel Comes with a House Key,* contains a brilliant discussion and many practical tips for the everyday practices we discussed.

Questions for My Discipler

Write down a few questions that you would like to talk about with your discipler.

Discipleship Session 14

☐ Prayer

Spend time together in prayer, invite the Holy Spirit to guide your conversation. Take a moment to sit in silence as you prepare to listen to God's leading.

☐ Celebration

What can you celebrate since you last met? How is God moving in your lives? What discipleship stories can you share?

☐ Review Previous Session

Take a moment to review the previous session. Are there any discussion points or items that you need to follow up on?

☐ Scripture

Read two passages of scripture from the ones used in the session. Choose one that encouraged and one that challenged you.

☐ God

What are the primary attributes that you learned about God's character in this section? What encouraged or challenged you?

☐ Yourself

What did you learn about yourself from the above passages?

☐ Obedience

Does what you learned change the way you think?

Does what you learned about change the way you act?

Does what you learned about change the way you treat others?

☐ Questions

Take a moment to talk through the questions you had.

☐ Next Step

What is one step you can take between now and your next session to practice what you learned?

Who can you share what you learned with to help them know Jesus?

☐ Pray

Share concerns. Pray for one another. Invite the Holy Spirit to help you.

☐ Next Discipleship Session _____

15

Sacrificial Living & Passion for the Lost

Welcome to your 15th discipleship session. This is the final session that will focus on missional living and the early church in Acts. We will specifically be looking at sacrificial living and developing a passion for the lost. Take a moment to praise Jesus for the many gifts and blessings in your life.

Scripture Reading

To help you prepare, read the following scriptures on your own:

- ☐ Acts 2:42-47
- ☐ Colossians 3:2
- ☐ Philippians 4:12
- ☐ Luke 15
- ☐ Luke 19:10

Respond

Make a list below in response to these questions. How did you choose to live where you are living? What factors influenced who you are living with? Which of the factors were missional?

Everyday Practice 5: Sacrificial Living

Acts 2:45

They sold their possessions and property and distributed the proceeds to all, as any had need.

We tend to view our successes as belonging to us. However, in a missional life, our possessions are merely a tool to be used for the glory of Jesus. In church circles, we regularly teach that our possessions are not our own. However, we must contextualize this teaching in light of the broader call to live a missional life. Without applying missional thinking to our possessions, we can give intellectual assent to the idea that our possessions belong to Jesus, but live in exactly the same manner as if they did not. In a missional mindset, our possessions are tools to advance the mission.

In the economy of God, our temporary possessions are transformed into tools that can build something of eternal value. It is a beautiful and wonderful privilege that we can use what we have for the glory of God.

Such strategic thinking may mean that we purchase a cheaper house, drive less expensive cars or take transit, or eat more economical food so that we can leverage our resources for the Kingdom. It may mean we do not go on as many vacations. It may mean that we do not take the promotion that we have worked hard to earn as it will consume more time.

At first glance, limiting our experiences or possessions sounds restrictive, but in fact, it is tremendously liberating. We are trading the temporary for the eternal in these moments. We are rejecting the lies of our culture that new experiences and better possessions are the key to a fulfilled life, and instead choosing to find our satisfaction in Jesus.

It may also mean that we work extra hard at work to gain the bonus so that we can invest it into the Kingdom. In either case, we do not labour for our benefit; we labour for the benefit of others and the name of Jesus. In missional living, the driving motivation for what we do with our possessions is maximizing Kingdom impact, not personal success or comfort. The temptations of worldliness can so easily hijack our attention, and we must continually return to Paul's words:

Colossians 3:2

Set your minds on things above, not on earthly things

In Paul's instruction to set our minds on Christ in Colossians 3, he highlights earthly tendencies that derail us: impurity, lust, evil desires and greed. Notably, he specifies that greed is a form of idolatry. We can identify the idols in our lives by evaluating what, should we lose it, would result in discontentment in our lives (Philippians 4:12). When our contentment, satisfaction and joy is found in Jesus, and in inviting others to know him, we no longer require more to be satisfied. By giving up what we have so that others can know Jesus, we are declaring that Jesus is our King and we are not beholden to the idol of material success.

Respond

How much energy do you spend chasing worldly pursuits (money, job, career and so forth)? How could you shift your thinking to eternal things?

Do you treat your possessions as your own or as tools the Lord has given you to bless others and to glorify Him? How do you know? List some examples below.

In what ways is your focus primarily on investing into the Kingdom? In what ways do you focus primarily on serving yourself?

Read Psalm 73. Do you relate to the envy of the Psalmist? Where does he ultimately find hope? Where do you ultimately find hope?

Sacrificial living means that we create three types of space in our lives: financial space, emotional space and calendar space.

Financial Space

Part of living sacrificially is creating financial margin in our lives so that we have the financial resources to bless others. Sacrificial living is not the same principle as radical generosity, although they are related. Sacrificial living is about structuring and building our lives so that as many people as possible will find hope in the Gospel. Radical generosity is about learning to give our time, talents and treasure to advance the Kingdom. Sacrificial living is about structuring and designing our lives to have less, whereas radical generosity is about giving to be a blessing. Consequently, sacrificial living lays the groundwork on which we can build radical generosity.

In an entirely practical sense, consumer debt is the death knell of sacrificial living. Debt is the practice of stealing from our future missionality to pay for our present greed. Sacrificial living is the practice of investing in our future missionality by giving up our present desires.

Part of creating financial space is intentionally living with less so that we do not have to spend all of our energy trying to financially sustain a standard of living or pursue greater possessions. Creating financial space means that we consider the cost of our possessions, homes, jobs and careers to our missionality.

Mental and Emotional Space

The text in Acts 2 highlights that the church gave *"as they had need."* Being aware of others' needs is actually a part of sacrificial living. By default, we tend to think first about ourselves, our wants, interests and hobbies. We are easily consumed with all sorts of mental or emotional addictions that limit our ability to serve and love others. These addictions include social media, television, sports and so forth. These things are not inherently evil, but we can very quickly become obsessed with them such that they consume an unhealthy amount of our mental and emotional capacity. Part of creating mental and emotional space means that we can be sensitive to others' needs. We structure our lives so that we intentionally have space to think about others instead of ourselves.

Calendar Space

Lastly, part of sacrificial living is to live simple, humble lives where we live to serve others. It means that we do not busy ourselves furthering our own interests, passions, careers and hobbies all the time. Instead, we structure our lives so that there is space for the needs of others. Physical space, of course, will fall into this category through the previous principals of intentional proximity and open home.

Respond

How much consumer (non-school) debt are you carrying? How could you pay it off sooner to be more missional? How can you be intentional about avoiding (non-school) debt in the future? Discuss with your discipler.

Would you be willing to limit your income level but work harder so that you could invest in the Kingdom and others?

How much of your "brain space" or "emotional space" is spent thinking about social media, television, games, sports or other areas of consuming? What could you eliminate to create more emotional space for caring for others? What steps can you take to ensure that you follow through with this commitment?

What is one area in which you are living on more than you really need? Perhaps driving a nicer car, renting a nicer apartment or eating out often. How could you simplify your life so that you can give more to others?

Everyday Practice 6: Passion for the Lost

Acts 2:47

Every day the Lord added to their number those who were being saved.

The final statement that described the early church in Acts is that they were regularly seeing people discover the saving grace of Jesus. The final statement here about the church is not anecdotal to the description of the church; rather, it is the end towards which everything else was pointing. The church passionately exists to see people know Jesus. They engaged their world with the Gospel and were regularly and consistently engaging people who did not yet know Jesus ("in the temple courts").

This final everyday practice of a missional life is of paramount importance. A missional life is all about seeing people know Jesus! The church was passionate about seeing people discover the hope of Jesus. They understood, at a very fundamental level, that the church does not exist to create a community, but rather the church exists to see the dead brought to life! Although, as discussed above, the community is an essential component of effectively living that mission, it is not the objective in and of itself.

The desire to see the lost know Jesus means that we must be regularly in contact with people who do not know Jesus. Our proximity with the church is a tool that allows us to invite those who do not know Jesus into contact with those who do. Our open home is a tool to welcome people who do not know Jesus into our lives so they can meet him. Our sacrificial living is a tool to demonstrate our profound freedom from consumerism and selfishness and invite people to a life of joyful generosity in Christ.

In a missional life, absolutely every component of our lives exists to see people know Jesus. We do not live our lives for ourselves; we live our lives so that people will know Jesus. We must resist the desire to create insulated Christian communities. We must be in the world, actively engaging it and proclaiming the simple Gospel message: that in Christ, we can be raised from death in sin to new life, by the grace of Jesus. Missional living and Gospel multiplication go hand-in-hand; they are inseparable. We know we are effectively living missionally if we are multiplying new disciples of Jesus, who, in turn, are multiplying new disciples of Jesus.

What does passion for the lost look like? In Luke 15, Jesus powerfully invites us to a life of passionate pursuit of those who are lost, using the three parables of the lost sheep, the lost coin and the lost son. In the parable of the lost sheep, Jesus emphasizes the value of reaching a single lost person, weighed against the security of the masses. Passion for the lost means that instead of remaining in the safety of a Christian bubble, we are compelled to go and see even just a single person come to know Jesus. The community must exist for the sake of the mission, not the mission for the community.

In the parable of the lost coin, the woman who has lost a coin carefully and intentionally rearranges her life to find the lost coin. She takes responsibility and invests time, energy and resources to see the coin found. Passion for the lost means an intentional, dedicated and concerted effort to see people know Jesus. Passion is not accidental. It requires us to rearrange the furniture of our lives to see lost people found, to use the metaphor of the parable.

In the parable of the lost son, passion for the lost is exhibited through the humility to receive people into the Kingdom as brothers and sisters. Despite the lost son's rebellion, his sin and the harm he caused to others, he was received as a son by his father. His reception as a son is crucial because it means that lost people are not less than those of us who have already found Jesus — they are those who may be invited to the Kingdom as brothers and sisters. We must be vigilant to the subtle pride that can arise in thinking that somehow those of us who have found Jesus are more valued, inherently holy or naturally righteous because we have already found Jesus. We were all lost before we found Jesus, or rather before Jesus found us. Consequently, our position towards the lost arises from compassion, love and kindness. We desire the lost to be found because we have ourselves been found and we know the life that is found in Jesus.

Weaved through the narratives of all three parables is a picture of rejoicing and celebration at the finding of a soul. Passion for the lost is expressed as joy when those who are found discover the hope of Jesus. It is no mere accident or fluke that people are resurrected to a new life in Christ. It is a profound and glorious testament to the goodness and loving-kindness of a God who sought us out, died for us, saved us and has invited us to be home in his presence.

Respond

How much time, energy and resources are you personally investing in seeing people who do not yet know Jesus find him?

Have you allowed any pride to creep in that says, "I'm better because I know Jesus"? Be honest and discuss your motivations for wanting people who do not know Jesus to know him with your discipler.

Have you found yourself in a "Christian bubble"? Have you allowed yourself to become too comfortable, spending all your time with Christians instead of connecting Christians and non-Christians together?

Who in your life is not yet a follower of Jesus? How can you be more intentional about serving these people and modelling the love of Jesus to them?

Summary

Missional living is all about intentionally structuring our lives so that people discover Jesus through them. In these final two everyday practices, we discovered:

- The importance of living a simple, humble life, free of the encumbrances of our culture.
- The importance of avoiding both debt and accumulating possessions.
- Nothing we have is really ours; it is all a tool so that we can be a blessing.
- We must create emotional and mental space by limiting our time spent consuming entertainment.
- We must intentionally invest energy, time and resources so that people know Jesus.
- We must be cautious of pride, in thinking that we are better because we know Jesus.
- We must be aware of when we are becoming too comfortable in a Christian bubble.

Further Scripture Reading

If you would like to read more scripture on the topics in this session, please read:

- ☐ Luke 19:1-10
- ☐ Luke 22:14
- ☐ Acts 2:1-4
- ☐ Mark 1:29-31

Questions for My Discipler

Write down a few questions that you would like to talk about with your discipler.

Discipleship Session 15

☐ Prayer

Spend time together in prayer, invite the Holy Spirit to guide your conversation. Take a moment to sit in silence as you prepare to listen to God's leading.

☐ Celebration

What can you celebrate since you last met? How is God moving in your lives? What discipleship stories can you share?

☐ Review Previous Session

Take a moment to review the previous session. Are there any discussion points or items that you need to follow up on?

☐ Scripture

Read two passages of scripture from the ones used in the session. Choose one that encouraged and one that challenged you.

☐ God

What are the primary attributes that you learned about God's character in this section? What encouraged or challenged you?

☐ Yourself

What did you learn about yourself from the above passages?

☐ Obedience

Does what you learned change the way you think?

Does what you learned about change the way you act?

Does what you learned about change the way you treat others?

☐ Questions

Take a moment to talk through the questions you had.

☐ Next Step

What is one step you can take between now and your next session to practice what you learned?

Who can you share what you learned with to help them know Jesus?

☐ Pray

Share concerns. Pray for one another. Invite the Holy Spirit to help you.

☐ Next Discipleship Session _____

Part 4

Radical Generosity

16
Radical Generosity

Welcome to your 16th discipleship session. This is the first of three sessions that will focus on radical generosity. We will specifically be looking at how radical generosity is a reflection of the gospel and asking the question, "What's 'radical' about radical generosity?" Take a moment to praise Jesus for giving his life for you.

Scripture Reading

To help you prepare, read the following scriptures on your own:

- ☐ Mark 10
- ☐ Matthew 10:8
- ☐ Ephesians 1:7-9
- ☐ 2 Corinthians 9:7-12
- ☐ 1 Corinthians 9:19,22-23

Respond

What stands out to you about the generosity of God, as shown in Jesus? How would you describe God's generosity?

Radical Generosity

When we think of the word generosity, we tend to think of finances or resources. While that is an essential component, true generosity is about so much more than just our finances — it includes our time and talents, as well.

Ephesians 5:25

Christ loved the church and gave himself for her.

Radical generosity, at its core, is an invitation to embody the nature of the Gospel by giving away that which is precious to us. The Gospel is the news about how God entered into a world that had utterly rejected him, and freely and intentionally gave all of himself to see us restored to life and relationship with him (Ephesians 5:25; Philippians 2:7). God is an outrageously radically generous God, who loves to give of himself to bless his creation. The invitation to radical generosity, then, is nothing short of an invitation to embody the character of Jesus.

Our generosity starts with gratitude, or worship, in response to

Radical Generosity Cycle

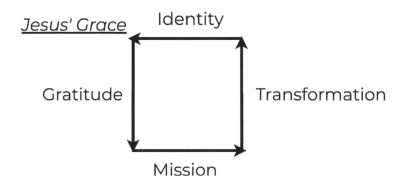

the Gospel. When we see that the Gospel is about how God gave himself, we cannot help but respond in worship. From that place of worship, we will want to see others also discover the hope of Jesus, and see our own lives transformed so that we live with missional generosity, as the previous diagram illustrates.

Our giving, in response to the Gospel, will naturally begin to transform us, which, in turn, leads us back to building a secure identity in Jesus. In other words, when we are generous, it naturally reinforces our understanding of the Gospel, our identity in Christ and the effectiveness of the mission of our lives.

> *[Jesus] is the most magnanimous of captains. If there is anything gracious, generous, kind and tender, lavish, and superabundant in love, you always find it in him. These forty years and more I have served him, and I have nothing but love for him. His service is life, peace, joy. Oh, that you would enter it at once! God help you to enlist under the banner of Jesus even this day.*[24]
> — **Charles Spurgeon**

Generosity, especially financially, gets to the heart of who we are and is one of the hardest areas in which to yield lordship to Jesus. Jesus places tremendous emphasis on financial generosity, because he recognizes how intertwined our souls can be with giving. Why does he speak about money so often? The answer is simple: your finances are a reflection of your heart (Matthew 6:21). Jesus desires authority over your whole heart, and if you are not willing to trust him with your finances, then he cannot have his way in your life. Here are just a few instances where Jesus addresses generosity:

> *Matthew 6:21; Matthew 6:24; Luke 3:14; Matthew 19:21; Matthew 21:12-13; Luke 12:33; Matthew 6:1-4; Matthew 12:41-44; Luke 14:28; Luke 16:13-15; Matthew 13:22; Matthew 13:44; Matthew 17:24-27; Mark 10:17-27; Mark 11:15-18; Luke 10:29-37*

In one particularly powerful encounter in Mark 10, Jesus engages a rich man who is yearning to discover the abundant life of God. He asks Jesus what he must do to achieve it, and Jesus responds by instructing him to give everything he has away. Jesus is inviting us to discover a profound principle: when we cling to our lives, financial or otherwise, it is a sickness that robs us of our life. The antidote for this sickness is simply radical, unqualified generosity.

Respond

Have you considered that generosity, of any kind, is a reflection of Jesus' lordship and obedience in our lives?

In what ways is the generosity in your life reflective of the generosity that God has shown you?

What does it mean to you that our generosity is a "reflection of the Gospel?"

What's so "radical"?

When we speak of radical generosity, it is important to define exactly what we mean by "radical." Generosity, of course, exists across the entire human experience. There are people who do not know Jesus who are very generous. However, radical generosity is generosity that is shaped and influenced by the Gospel in at least seven specific ways.

1) Costly

Firstly, the generosity exhibited in the Gospel is profoundly costly. As Philippians 2:8 says, Jesus emptied himself, giving up everything to enter our world and suffer and die for us. 1 John 4:9 highlights that the Father gave that which was the most precious to him: his only Son. Radical generosity is not stingy, piecemeal or safe generosity. It is costly and often risky. It will mean that we will have to give up that which is precious to us. However, part of radical generosity is that we give without fear because we know that God is our ultimate provider.

2) Independent of Past Performance

Secondly, radical generosity is independent of past performance. While we were still sinners, Christ died for us (Romans 5:8; Colossians 1:21)! God's radical generosity towards us was in spite of the fact that we had done absolutely nothing to earn it. We found ourselves as enemies of God, yet he chose to restore relationship proactively. A generosity that is attached to performance is not generosity; it is just payment.[25]

3) Given Freely

Thirdly, radical generosity is given freely, without strings attached. When Jesus commissioned the disciples for ministry, he said to them:

Matthew 10:8

Freely you have received; freely give.

In Luke 6:35, Jesus affirms that we should give without expecting anything in return. In his address to the Athenians, Paul affirms that we could never repay God for his generosity (Acts 17:25), yet God gave himself anyway. When we give, we do not give so that we can get in return. Rather, we give freely because we have already freely received. This is equally true when we give to God as when we give to those around us. Just as we do not tithe or give to God in order to receive a blessing, we likewise do not give to those around us in order to receive something in return. This does not apply just to receiving finances — we must give freely without looking to receive acclaim, status or even thanks and appreciation. Jesus gave himself freely for many who don't appreciate that sacrifice.

4) Intentional

Fourthly, it is intentional. Radical generosity is not random or without wisdom. Listen to how Paul describes the wisdom of God in the Gospel:

Ephesians 1:7-9

In him we have redemption through his blood, the forgiveness of our trespasses, according to the riches of his grace that he richly poured out on us with all wisdom and understanding. He made known to us the mystery of his will, according to his good pleasure that he purposed in Christ.

Not only was the Gospel tremendously costly, free and without strings, it was also wise and preplanned! Radical generosity will be generosity that seeks to maximize its impact. One word of caution: wisdom when dispensing radical generosity will not be the wisdom of the world but instead must be patterned after the wisdom of God as revealed in the previous three discipleship emphases.

Further, intentionality means that we do not simply wait around for opportunities to be generous or for significant needs to pop up. Instead, we must actively and intentionally seek out avenues to practice radical generosity in the world around us.

5) Joyful

Fifthly, radical generosity is joyful! We are called in 2 Corinthians 9:7 to give with a joyful and eager heart. Radical generosity is the natural and joyful overflow of people who have encountered the radical generosity of God! Giving of ourselves is a privilege and should bring us joy. In fact, Hebrews 12:2 states that it was joy that motivated Jesus to sacrifice himself on the cross for us. The result of Jesus' sacrifice was joy, both for us as well as for Jesus! Radical generosity that is modelled after Jesus produces joy in us. Notice that this is the opposite of pride, bitterness or arrogance that would result from selfish "generosity." Holy Spirit led generosity will always produce the fruit of joy in our hearts (Acts 2:46).

6) Requires all of us

Sixthly, radical generosity requires all of us. Often the question is asked, "Where do we start when implementing radical generosity?" The answer is simple, yet demanding: we start with all of our lives. We must give all of ourselves to the cause of Christ. If Jesus is Lord and his mission is our mission, then our entire life must be given to that cause.

1 Corinthians 9:19,22-23

Although I am free from all and not anyone's slave, I have made myself a slave to everyone, in order to win more people… I have become all things to all people, so that I may by every possible means save some. Now I do all this because of the gospel, so that I may share in the blessings.

In this way, radical generosity is the natural extension of missional living. In being invited to give our lives, we are invited to exhaust our lives for the benefit of others that they may know Jesus (Philippians 2:17). Radical generosity is indeed quite radical in that we are being invited to give all of ourselves to the cause of Christ — not just a part of ourselves or portion of our lives. There is no better way that we can spend our lives. We are called to lower ourselves so that we can lift others up. In doing so, we adopt the posture of a servant or slave so that we see others raised to life. The Gospel invites us to give all of our lives for the benefit of others. To restate this clearly: we do not live our lives to benefit ourselves. We live our lives for the cause of Christ and the service of others (Matthew 20:27-28).

7) Invitation to Partnership

Lastly, the invitation to radical generosity is directly connected to and expressed as an invitation to partner with the mission of God in this world. In this way, our generosity is an active partnership as we invest into what God is already doing in the world.

2 Corinthians 9:11-12

You will be enriched in every way to be generous in every way, which through us will produce thanksgiving to God. For the ministry of this service is not only supplying the needs of the saints but is also overflowing in many thanksgivings to God.

In both the Old and the New Testament, financial giving served the purpose of supporting, sustaining and advancing what God was doing through his people. God is always moving, and when he moves, it is always through people. Through financial giving, we are given the privilege of partnering with what God is doing in our church, our city and our nation.

God's desire to use disciples to build his church can be seen in 2 Corinthians 9, as Paul invites the church to continue the mission of the local church by "supplying the needs of the saints." In Numbers 18, the Levites also depended upon the contributions of the people to facilitate worship in the tabernacle. The people of God have always been called to invest in the broader things that God is doing in the world, with our time, talents and treasures. It is a supreme joy that we, the people of God, are always invited to the opportunity to partner with the mission of God through our radical generosity.

Giving to the Kingdom of God is very different from giving to a charitable cause, because we are invited to practice it in the context of our church family. We are not just throwing our gifts over the fence and hoping for the best. Rather, we give with radical generosity as participants and co-labourers. We give as a part of a much bigger whole, not as disconnected investors who are relationally disinterested in the outcomes. The call to radical generosity is part of a broader call to be an active participant in the purpose of the Kingdom. Giving is just one component of the beautiful truth that we are called to be a contributor to the Kingdom of God.

Respond

Which of the 7 aspects of radical generosity do you find the easiest? Which one do you find the hardest? Why?

How could you be more intentionally generous with non-financial aspects of your life such as with your words, gifts or hospitality?

When you give to others, do you expect a gift in return? When you receive a gift, do you feel obligated to give in return? Why do you think that is? Discuss with your discipler.

Is giving financially to the church easier or more difficult than giving to a charity? Why or why not? Do you understand why it is so important to give to your church family? Is this a new concept for you? How does this change the way that you think about giving financially?

Summary

Radical generosity is generosity that is modelled by the Gospel. Just as Jesus freely gave himself for our benefit, so we give our lives for the benefit of others. Radical generosity challenges a few parts of our thinking:

- Radical generosity is a matter of Jesus' lordship in our lives.
- Radical generosity has 7 attributes:
  - Costly
  - Independent of past performance
  - Freely given
  - Intentional
  - Joyful
  - Requires all of us
  - Is an invitation to partnership

Further Scripture Reading

If you would like to read more scripture on the topics in this session, please read:

- ☐ Acts 17:25
- ☐ Luke 6:35
- ☐ Romans 5:8
- ☐ Ephesians 5:25
- ☐ Philippians 2:7-17

Questions for My Discipler

Write down a few questions that you would like to talk about with your discipler.

Discipleship Session 16

☐ Prayer

Spend time together in prayer, invite the Holy Spirit to guide your conversation. Take a moment to sit in silence as you prepare to listen to God's leading.

☐ Celebration

What can you celebrate since you last met? How is God moving in your lives? What discipleship stories can you share?

☐ Review Previous Session

Take a moment to review the previous session. Are there any discussion points or items that you need to follow up on?

☐ Scripture

Read two passages of scripture from the ones used in the session. Choose one that encouraged and one that challenged you.

☐ God

What are the primary attributes that you learned about God's character in this section? What encouraged or challenged you?

☐ Yourself

What did you learn about yourself from the above passages?

☐ Obedience

Does what you learned change the way you think?

Does what you learned about change the way you act?

Does what you learned about change the way you treat others?

☐ Questions

Take a moment to talk through the questions you had.

☐ Next Step

What is one step you can take between now and your next session to practice what you learned?

Who can you share what you learned with to help them know Jesus?

☐ Pray

Share concerns. Pray for one another. Invite the Holy Spirit to help you.

☐ Next Discipleship Session _____

17
Time & Talent

Welcome to your 17th discipleship session. This is the second of three sessions that will focus on radical generosity. Take a moment to thank the Lord for the gift of spending time with him.

Scripture Reading

To help you prepare, read the following scriptures on your own:

- [ ] Psalm 90:12
- [ ] Galatians 6:10
- [ ] 1 Peter 4:10
- [ ] 1 Corinthians 12:1-11
- [ ] Romans 12:6-8

Respond

What stands out to you about the generosity of God, as shown in Jesus? How would you describe God's generosity?

Time

The first area of our lives with which we can be radically generous is our time. If Jesus is Lord of all of our lives, then the natural application is that Jesus is Lord over all of our time. All time is Jesus' time. Every second we have is a gift from him, and we have a responsibility to steward that gift of time effectively. Just as missional living is about the integration of every aspect of our lives to advance the Gospel, radical generosity with our time is about learning to see that Jesus is Lord over all of our time. As a result, we give our time to him and do not hoard it for ourselves. Our time is one of the most precious gifts that we can give away. We only have a limited quantity of it, and once it is spent, we cannot get any more. It is a very limited resource, which is why it can be so hard to give it away.

Radical generosity with our time is giving our time away to benefit others ahead of ourselves. One of the primary ways we can give our time away is in the act of serving others as Jesus commands us in Matthew 20:27. While serving others — putting their needs ahead of ours — is one of the best ways that we can be generous, it will, however, require that we give time regularly. The act of serving cannot be a one-off or occasional activity but must be an intentional, costly and freely given gift for the benefit of others.

Radical generosity with our time is about so much more than merely adding volunteerism to our already hectic lives. As mentioned earlier, radical generosity is intentional. As such, being generous with our time requires that we intentionally build our lives so that we can be as generous with our time as possible. We may not be as gifted as others or have as many resources, but every single person has time that they can be generous with. We are all allocated the same 24 hours per day. What would it look like if we desired to be as generous as possible with the time we have been given?

We often approach generosity with a fear that if we give away that which is precious, we will not have enough. One of the primary areas where this occurs is in our time; we can eagerly hoard it for ourselves as if it was ours. As the Gospel transforms us and we adopt the identity of a servant, the desire to give our time away will build in us, and it will become as natural as breathing. It is true that radical generosity with our time may mean that we have less time for ourselves or our preferred activities. However, as we learn to give, our desires will change, as Psalm 90:12 highlights.

Psalm 90:12

Teach us to number our days carefully so that we may develop wisdom in our hearts.

Serving the Church

We can contextualize the need to be generous with our time in the local church as the instruction in Galatians summarizes. For this reason, we encourage people to serve the church and join in the mission by giving their time. The invitation to give our time will likely mean that we have to surrender our schedules to Jesus and allow him to bless us with the time resources that we need to accomplish all that he has entrusted us.

Galatians 6:10

Therefore, as we have opportunity, let us work for the good of all, especially for those who belong to the household of faith.

The invitation to radical generosity in our teams means that we need to rethink what it means to "work for the church." Churches have historically been operated by professional clergy. However, with all of the above comments regarding missional living and radical generosity, it should be abundantly clear that we all work for the church. We may or may not be paid to do so, but that is of relatively minor consequence. The real question we should be asking is not one of pay but one of structure: *"How can I structure my life so that I can generously invest it in the purposes of the Kingdom?"*

Respond

Are you hesitant to share your time with those you are in discipleship relationships with? How much time and energy are you investing into discipling others?

Do you currently see yourself as "working for the church" or just "volunteering"? Would you say that you are a diligent worker?

What are the primary hesitations you have in serving others with your time? Discuss these with your discipler.

Would you be willing to serve in a way that you are not naturally gifted, simply because there is a need or an opportunity? Why or why not?

Talents and Gifts

The second component of radical generosity is generosity with our talents and spiritual gifts. Jesus has given every single disciple both natural and supernatural gifts. However, these gifts are not for our benefit; they are for the benefit of the mission of the church and the name of Jesus.

Our natural gifts are given to us so that we can serve others, not ourselves. When it comes to our talents, we should be eager to give our best to the glory of God. Often, we will give Jesus what is left after we have first leveraged our talents for ourselves. What would it look like if we gave our best to the cause of Christ? Jesus has given us specific natural gifts so that we can use them to serve the mission of God, not just ourselves!

1 Peter 4:10

Based on the gift they have received, everyone should use it to serve others, as good managers of the varied grace of God.

For our individual talents, we get the privilege and the joy of asking how we can use them to further the mission of Jesus. So often, talented and gifted Christians are sidelined from active ministry because their gifts do not fit a stereotypical mould of what church ministry "should" look like. In reality, the church should have all the diversity in gifting that we see more broadly, because we are made up of all people! What would it look like to take the things we are most gifted at and most passionate about, and to surrender them to Jesus with an attitude that says, "These are yours, use them for your glory"?

Radical generosity with our gifts means that we do not expect or desire recognition for our giving. We do not seek praise. Radical generosity means that the primary objective of giving our gifts is to be a blessing, rather than accruing spiritual credit.

It can be tempting to believe that disciple-makers require a magical "it factor" or some form of "cool" that causes them to gain followers naturally. A disciple-maker is not a leader who attracts followers by force of their personality but one who mobilizes those who are around them for greater impact. Disciple-making is all about activating others for mission, not building a following around ourselves. The job of the discipler, as described in Ephesians 4, is to equip others for ministry, not to do it all themselves.

Our job as disciples, based on the gifts God has given us, is to disciple and encourage others to go and make their own disciples. We are all gifted for this task!

Supernatural Gifts

Just as we should be generous with our natural talents, we likewise need to practice radical generosity with our spiritual gifts. Scripture is abundantly clear that the Holy Spirit supernaturally empowers every believer in a specific way:

1 Corinthians 12:7

A manifestation of the Spirit is given to each person for the common good

The phrase "to each person" means precisely what it says; everyone has been given a gift. The generosity of our God extends past the sacrifice of Jesus to the invitation and empowerment to join him in his mission! However, the temptation is to think that these supernatural talents and gifts give us a special, heightened spiritual pedigree. Such an attitude is categorically false.

The gifts the Spirit has given us have absolutely nothing to do with us, and they certainly do not exist for our benefit. We are given gifts, as the above scripture clearly states, "For the common good." Said another way, we have been given a spiritual gift so that we can freely and generously give it away — so that we can bless and build up the body of Christ! Paul briefly highlights this in 1 Corinthians 12:7-11 and Romans 12:6-8.

1 Corinthians 12:7-11

To one is given a message of wisdom through the Spirit, to another, a message of knowledge by the same Spirit, to another, faith by the same Spirit, to another, gifts of healing by the one Spirit, to another, the performing of miracles, to another, prophecy, to another, distinguishing between spirits, to another, different kinds of tongues, to another, interpretation of tongues. One and the same Spirit is active in all these, distributing to each person as he wills.

Romans 12:6-8

According to the grace given to us, we have different gifts: If prophecy, use it according to the proportion of one's faith; if service, use it in service; if teaching, in teaching; if exhorting, in exhortation; giving, with generosity; leading, with diligence; showing mercy, with cheerfulness.

Spiritual and natural gifts are both a work of grace in our lives; they are radically generous gifts from a good and loving God that reflect his character and the Gospel itself. God has blessed us as an outworking of his grace, not as a reward for our work or as an indication of how special we are. The Holy Spirit gives them because our God is a generous God who loves to bless his people. Spiritual gifts are given to us with the same seven properties of radical generosity that we highlighted in the last chapter. As a result, we should desire and use our spiritual gifts with a posture of radical generosity, eager to see the Lord bless us so that we can be a blessing to others.

Respond

Do you believe that God has uniquely made you to be a blessing to others by giving you special gifts that you can give away? Why or why not?

What gifts can you identify in yourself that you have been given and how are you using these to be generous in God's Kingdom?

Do you desire praise when you serve people with your time or talents, even subconsciously? Discuss the possible roots of this (such as pride or insecurity) with your discipler.

Have you, as Paul instructs, earnestly desired a supernatural gift (1 Corinthians 14:1)? Why or why not? Pray with your discipler that the Holy Spirit would give you gifts so you can be a blessing to others and build the church.

What gifts do you see in those you are discipling? Have you identified this "gold" in them and called it out in them? Do you have a habit of actively seeking to see the best in the people you are discipling? Why or why not?

Summary

Radical generosity with our time, talents and supernatural gifts is an important application of radical generosity. We learned that:

- Generosity with our time can be particularly challenging but is particularly important.
- We all "work for the Church" in the sense that our primary calling is to invest our lives into building the Kingdom of God, not our own personal kingdoms.
- Each of us has been given natural and supernatural gifts so that we can be a blessing to others.
- It is important that we believe that every person has been given gifts for disciple-making.
- We must not hoard our gifts for ourselves.
- We must watch out that our hearts do not desire praise for ourselves when we serve with our gifts or time.

Further Scripture Reading

If you would like to read more scripture on the topics in this session, please read:

- ☐ Matthew 20:27
- ☐ 1 Corinthians 14:1-10
- ☐ Ephesians 4:1-16

Questions for My Discipler

Write down a few questions that you would like to talk about with your discipler.

Discipleship Session 17

☐ Prayer

Spend time together in prayer, invite the Holy Spirit to guide your conversation. Take a moment to sit in silence as you prepare to listen to God's leading.

☐ Celebration

What can you celebrate since you last met? How is God moving in your lives? What discipleship stories can you share?

☐ Review Previous Session

Take a moment to review the previous session. Are there any discussion points or items that you need to follow up on?

☐ Scripture

Read two passages of scripture from the ones used in the session. Choose one that encouraged and one that challenged you.

☐ God

What are the primary attributes that you learned about God's character in this section? What encouraged or challenged you?

☐ Yourself

What did you learn about yourself from the above passages?

☐ Obedience

Does what you learned change the way you think?

Does what you learned about change the way you act?

Does what you learned about change the way you treat others?

☐ Questions

Take a moment to talk through the questions you had.

☐ Next Step

What is one step you can take between now and your next session to practice what you learned?

Who can you share what you learned with to help them know Jesus?

☐ Pray

Share concerns. Pray for one another. Invite the Holy Spirit to help you.

☐ Next Discipleship Session _____

18
Treasure

Welcome to your 18th discipleship session. This is the final session that will focus on radical generosity. We will specifically be focusing on radical generosity in our finances. Take a moment to thank God for his provision in your life.

Scripture Reading

To help you prepare, read the following scriptures on your own:

☐ 1 Timothy 6:17-18
☐ 2 Corinthians 9:6-12
☐ 1 John 2:15-17
☐ Proverbs 3:9

Respond

When you get income or money, what is the very first thing that you do with it?

Treasures

The final area of radical generosity is with our treasure: our finances. As mentioned in the introduction to radical generosity, finances represent a major thrust of Jesus' teaching. In fact, he teaches on the dangers of wealth and the need to be generous more than any other subject. Jesus' emphasis is in large part because money is at the very heart of who we are:

Matthew 6:21

For where your treasure is, there your heart will be also.

Without question, there is a clear and compelling invitation to radical financial generosity painted in the scriptures. It is expanded from Jesus' teaching and reiterated by the apostles in 2 Corinthians 9, 1 Timothy 6 and James 5. Radical financial generosity also has a significant emphasis in the narrative of the Old Testament. This includes Abraham (Genesis 12), the nation of Israel (Micah 3:10) and God's critiques of the pagan nations (Isaiah 47:8). God has made it abundantly clear that our financial blessing is ultimately not for ourselves. Instead, if we have been blessed financially, we have the joy and responsibility of giving it away.

1 Timothy 6:17-18

Instruct those who are rich in the present age not to be arrogant or to set their hope on the uncertainty of wealth, but on God, who richly provides us with all things to enjoy. Instruct them to do what is good, to be rich in good works, to be generous and willing to share

We may think that we do not have enough to be generous, but Jesus drives the important point home that all financial blessing, no matter how small, has been given so that we can bless others. The story of the poor widow giving everything she has in Luke 21:1-3 powerfully illustrates this point.

Respond

Have you seriously evaluated biblical teaching on finances, as listed above? Where would you say your current practices align with what is taught in scripture? Where do they not align?

Do you believe that God is your provider, not yourself? Why or why not?

Have you had a conversation about finances with the person you are discipling? How have you seen the position of money in their life? Are they in a place of health or a place of danger? How can you encourage and challenge them to grow in their dependence upon God through their finances?

A Generous Attitude

A joyful and eager heart should accompany our generosity (2 Corinthians 9:7). However, this should not mean that we need to wait until our heart is happy to give in order to begin the practice of giving. If that were the case, we would likely never learn to be radically generous. Instead, if our heart is struggling with giving, we should pray that the Lord would provide us with a new heart! The very next verse in 2 Corinthians 9:8 highlights that our generosity is a reflection of the grace that we have received!

2 Corinthians 9:6-8

The point is this: The person who sows sparingly will also reap sparingly, and the person who sows generously will also reap generously. Each person should do as he has decided in his heart —not reluctantly or out of compulsion, since God loves a cheerful giver. And God is able to make every grace overflow to you, so that in every way, always having everything you need, you may excel in every good work.

Generous Desires

Our hearts yearn for all kinds of things, some of them useful and some of them selfish. Part of learning to live radically generous is training our hearts to seek after the things of God (Colossians 3:1-3). We must be intentional, and regularly submit our hearts to the words of Jesus and reject the temptations of the world. Every day, we are bombarded with thousands of messages that say we need more, deserve more and should get more. It is no wonder we continually feel as though we lack! We must counteract our culture by daily saturating our minds with the values of the Kingdom: in Christ we have everything we need, in Christ we are rich and through Christ we are satisfied. We need to train our minds and our hearts to reject worldliness and instead pursue pleasure in the love of the Father (1 John 2:15-17).

1 John 2:15-17

Do not love the world or the things in the world. If anyone loves the world, the love of the Father is not in him. For everything in the world—the lust of the flesh, the lust of the eyes, and the pride in one's possessions—is not from the Father, but is from the world. And the world with its lust is passing away, but the one who does the will of God remains forever.

As our hearts are increasingly satisfied in Christ and moulded after him, we will naturally begin to see the fruit of regular radical generosity in our lives. In this way, being radically generous with our finances will break the hold of anxiety about our finances. When we are discipling people and we encounter those who are anxious about financial provision, we can often anticipate an associated underdeveloped habit of generosity. The best way to invite people to discover freedom from anxiety about their finances is to invite them into the habit of regular, consistent giving.

Respond

Make a list of things that you really love. How many of them would you honestly say you love more than Christ? Ask your discipler for their input.

Would you say you have a joyful, grateful attitude towards giving? Why or why not?

If you knew that giving money away would reduce your anxiety about finances, would you be more generous? What is stopping you? How will this truth change the way you walk through conversations about our treasure with those you are discipling?

Do you feel as though you do not have "enough" to give? Would you be willing to take a leap and begin developing the habit? Discuss with your discipler.

Generous Practices

The tendency for our desires to drift from Christ is why giving must be a consistent and frequent part of our lives. Throughout scripture, this was often referred to as the tithe or first-fruits (Exodus 23:19). Radical generosity does not give from our leftovers; it is intentional and proactive. As with our time and talents, we are invited to give away the very best of our treasures.

Proverbs 3:9

Honour the LORD with your wealth and with the best part of everything you produce.

Tithing, which Jesus himself affirmed in Luke 11:42, is often referred to as giving the first 10% of our income. However, this is likely a low estimate based on the Old Testament patterns around tithing. 10% is not the goal, but rather it serves as a good starting point to practice generosity. The New Testament does not prescribe a particular quantity that we should give away, because all of it ultimately belongs to Jesus and exists for his glory. As a result, the goal is not to give away 10%. The goal is to give away as much as possible to see as many people as possible come to know the goodness and grace of Jesus.

In this way, the discipleship emphasis of radical generosity is built on the emphasis of missional living, especially the everyday practice of sacrificial living. The Lord has graciously invited us to a life of mission where we live and give our lives and resources so that others come to know Jesus. We get the privilege of living humbly to bless others. We do not need granite countertops, new cars, homeownership, fancy phones, vacations, new fashion-forward clothing or otherworldly things. We do not need them because we have everything we need in Christ for contentment. Moreover, we get to give them up and invest in something truly eternal: the body of Christ. What a supreme joy!

Muscle Practice

Radical generosity is a discipleship emphasis that takes practice to develop. Like a physical muscle, we must routinely and regularly exercise it to see it grow. To develop radical generosity, we need to start by structuring our time and finances so that we are positioned to give. Intentionally structuring our time and finances may mean putting aside activities or habits that are not productive for the Kingdom, or developing a proper financial plan. We must remember that radical generosity is intentional, and that means we must intentionally build and structure our lives so that we can practice giving in a radically generous way.

Respond

Are you set up to be radically generous with your finances? Do you have 1) a budget, 2) a savings plan and 3) no debt? (Download a budget guide at engage.liftchurch.ca)

Are you giving from the first income you receive, or from what is left over after you spend it? How much of your income are you giving away? How can you increase that amount? Why would you be hesitant to?

What can you sacrifice in your life so that you can be more generous? Perhaps a cheaper car, cell-phone plan, subscriptions or vacations.

What are some practical steps that you can take with at least one person who you are discipling to exercise their muscle in radical generosity? How can you take what you have learned in this chapter and teach them what it truly means to live lives of radical generosity?

Summary

Radical generosity is perhaps most easily evaluated through our finances. It is a major feature in scripture, and we should receive the call to be radically generous with joy. In this session, we discussed that:

- God is ultimately our provider, not us.

- As we give, we actually experience reduced anxiety as the grip of finances on our hearts is loosened.
- An attitude of joy is essential in giving; but rather than waiting for joy to come, we pray and invite the Holy Spirit to change our hearts while we start the habit.
- We can always give, no matter how little we have.
- Generosity must be intentional and proactive, not reactionary with our leftovers.
- Radical generosity takes practice to develop.

Further Scripture Reading

If you would like to read more scripture on the topics in this session, please read:

- ☐ Exodus 23:19
- ☐ Matthew 6:21
- ☐ James 5:1-9
- ☐ Micah 3:10
- ☐ Luke 21:1-3
- ☐ Luke 11:42

Additional Resources:

Download the Super Simple Budget guide under Discipleship Sources at engage.liftchurch.ca and work through it with your discipler to help you develop the habit of radical generosity.

Questions for My Discipler

Write down a few questions that you would like to talk about with your discipler.

Discipleship Session 18

☐ Prayer

Spend time together in prayer, invite the Holy Spirit to guide your conversation. Take a moment to sit in silence as you prepare to listen to God's leading.

☐ Celebration

What can you celebrate since you last met? How is God moving in your lives? What discipleship stories can you share?

☐ Review Previous Session

Take a moment to review the previous session. Are there any discussion points or items that you need to follow up on?

☐ Scripture

Read two passages of scripture from the ones used in the session. Choose one that encouraged and one that challenged you.

☐ God

What are the primary attributes that you learned about God's character in this section? What encouraged or challenged you?

☐ Yourself

What did you learn about yourself from the above passages?

☐ Obedience

Does what you learned change the way you think?

Does what you learned about change the way you act?

Does what you learned about change the way you treat others?

☐ Questions

Take a moment to talk through the questions you had.

☐ Next Step

What is one step you can take between now and your next session to practice what you learned?

Who can you share what you learned with to help them know Jesus?

☐ Pray

Share concerns. Pray for one another. Invite the Holy Spirit to help you.

☐ Next Discipleship Session _____

Part 5

Crucial Conversations

19
Crucial Conversations

Welcome to your 19th discipleship session. This is the first of four sessions that will focus on the final discipleship emphasis: crucial conversations. Take a moment to thank God for people who have encouraged you to follow Jesus!

Scripture Reading

To help you prepare, read the following scriptures on your own:

- [ ] John 1:14
- [ ] Ephesians 4:15
- [ ] 1 Peter 5:5
- [ ] 1 Corinthians 5:12

Respond

How do you personally handle feedback when you are emotionally healthy? What about when you are emotionally unhealthy?

Crucial Conversations

The final discipleship emphasis is crucial conversations. This is the discipleship emphasis which hones in on our ability to both lead and to be led in relationships with people — especially on matters of faith and life. The conversations and relationships in question could be between any mix of believers and unbelievers. While it may sound strange at first that our relational and conversational ability would be a discipleship issue, it is absolutely critical to discipleship. In order to see consistent growth in discipleship and multiplication for the Kingdom, it is essential that we can engage in discipleship conversations with substance, humility, conviction and boldness. Our relationship with Jesus is not a private issue; rather, our faith is always worked out publicly and in the context of our particular local church community (see *missional living*). Without the ability to receive and lead discipleship discussions, the Gospel cannot propagate — in us or in others. The Gospel, after all, is news about what has happened in Jesus, and news requires that someone proclaims it.

Our engagement in crucial conversations is a direct reflection of the depth of formation in the previous four discipleship emphases. As we grow in gospel fluency, secure identity, missional living and radical generosity, the conversations and relationships in our life will naturally begin to be shaped by them.

A crucial conversation is a conversation where we are either moving someone closer to an effective multiplying relationship with Jesus or one where we are being challenged to grow in our relationship with Jesus. Crucial conversations are a primary mechanism for both inner-life transformation and outer-life multiplication. On one hand, crucial conversations are the means by which the other discipleship emphases are formed in us, but they are also the means by which we multiply the discipleship emphases in others.

Crucial conversations are where we are confronted, and confront others, about the gaps between our words about Jesus and our actions. One of the greatest threats to our faith is when our ability to talk about Jesus is not reflected in our actions. Jesus is very clear that hypocrisy is a great evil that we must not tolerate (see Matthew 23). This is why crucial conversations are such an important aspect of discipleship, as highlighted in Ephesians 4:15; without the ability to challenge and be challenged in our walk with Jesus, we cannot see people mature to fullness in Christ.

Ephesians 4:15

But speaking the truth in love, let us grow in every way into him who is the head—Christ.

Respond

Have you thought of receiving input from your discipler and giving feedback to those you are discipling as a discipleship issue itself? Why or why not?

Are there any crucial conversations that someone needs to have with you? Be proactive and let your discipler know what's going on.

Are there any crucial conversations that you need to have with someone you are discipling? What is holding you back?

Grace and Truth

The invitation to engage in crucial conversations is a direct reflection of Jesus' own life. As John 1:14 states, and Jesus' ministry repeatedly evidences, Jesus came in grace and truth. Grace, because Jesus did not have to come and we did not deserve the gift of his life, death and resurrection. Truth, because we needed to be called to repentance as sinners in desperate need of a saviour; we were dead people in need of resurrection.

John 1:14

The Word became flesh and dwelt among us. We observed his glory, the glory as the one and only Son from the Father, full of grace and truth.

The Gospel itself is simultaneously the most gracious message on earth and the most truthful. The Gospel takes the human condition of our sinfulness tremendously seriously. We are dead in our sin and there is absolutely nothing we can do ourselves to change that fact. This is the profound truth attested to by the Gospel and reaffirmed throughout the scriptures — especially in the narrative of the Old Testament. The narrative of the continual rebellion of Israel against the loving kindness of God demonstrates both our sinfulness and our desperate need for a saviour. However, the Gospel is also grace; we have been raised to life in Jesus because of his great love for us. This incredible duality of grace and truth is woven throughout the Bible.

Jesus' own ministry is equally characterized by an invitation to receive the Kingdom of God (grace) and his direct challenge to turn around when people were not headed in the right direction (truth/repentance). Jesus calls the disciples to follow him (grace), but he also calls people to repentance (truth). We can see this duality in Matthew 4:

Matthew 4:17-19

From then on Jesus began to preach, "Repent, because the kingdom of heaven has come near." As he was walking along the Sea of Galilee, he saw two brothers, Simon, and his brother Andrew. They were casting a net into the sea—for they were fishermen. "Follow me," he told them, "and I will make you fish for people." Immediately they left their nets and followed him.

Another powerful example of Jesus inviting the disciples into deep relationship while also challenging them directly is found in Matthew 16. Jesus invites Peter to acknowledge who he is as the Messiah and subsequently celebrates Peter (Matthew 16:18). However, moments later, Jesus famously rebuked Peter for misunderstanding the impending crucifixion with the direct words, *"get behind me Satan"* (Matthew 16:20-23). It is a brilliant example of the grace and truth of Jesus being lived in a discipleship context.

We must model this duality ourselves when being discipled and discipling others. We must invite people to a deeper relationship with Jesus while challenging them in the areas that they are not submitting to Jesus. We must pattern all our discipleship conversations after Jesus' life of grace and truth — invitation and challenge. We must directly confront our sin, on the one hand, and, on the other hand, consistently point to the forgiveness and grace of Jesus.

It may appear that grace and truth exist in tension with one another, as if grace comes at the expense of truth or truth at the expense of grace, but this is not the case. Jesus came *full* of grace and *full* of truth. He was completely grace, and he was completely truth. A proper discipleship relationship will include both in concert together; grace and truth exist in a supporting relationship with each other in healthy multiplying discipleship relationships.

It is worth emphasizing that while moral issues may play an important role in crucial conversations, they do not represent the totality of the content. We must resist the urge to fatally reduce the Gospel to a moral code in which the "righteous" challenge and judge the sinner. The primary emphasis in our crucial conversations must be an invitation to embrace the fullness of the Gospel. In the same way that the Gospel sanctifies us and calls us to mission, crucial conversations are an invitation to personal transformation and a call to mission. Crucial conversations must speak to both our inner and outer life. The second component of outer-life challenge is equally as important as the inner-life aspects of our crucial conversations. In crucial conversations, the primary objective is to lead people to embrace the goodness of Jesus and his call on their life.

Respond

When you look at the way that Jesus taught, do you personally connect more with the grace aspects of Jesus or the truth aspects? Why do you think that is?

Have you tended to believe that you can either be "nice" or "right," but not both? How might thinking in terms of "grace" and "truth" better reconcile that tension?

How can you learn from Jesus' model of being fully grace and fully truth in your own discipleship relationships? How does this change the way that you view crucial conversations, in both receiving and in giving them?

Crucial Conversations with Believers

There are two essential ingredients when we approach crucial conversations with believers: humility and boldness. We require these ingredients on both the receiving side and the leading side of the conversation.

Receiving with Humility

First, we need a significant degree of humility when being on the receiving end of a crucial conversation. One of the most important character traits in a discipleship relationship is that of teachability. When we are on the receiving end of a challenge to our character, the temptation is to immediately get defensive and assume the person challenging us is wrong. There are few things that can derail our own discipleship journey as quickly as a defensive and unteachable spirit. Our discipleship journey is going to require a deep unearthing of our souls in order to see them more conformed to the person of Jesus. By its very nature, this process of discipleship will be uncomfortable and likely painful. While the Holy Spirit can, and regularly does, convict us directly through his leading and his Word, many of the direct challenges of our discipleship will occur in the context of a crucial conversation.

Humility is more than just receiving the challenge with eagerness and gratitude. Humility actually means that we will seek out the discipleship relationships knowing that we have work to do — we not only graciously receive input into our lives, but we intentionally seek it out! Discipleship is a two-way street in which the disciple must open their life up, inviting input, and the discipler must speak boldly. However, without the foundation of a willing and teachable attitude, the discipleship process will be difficult to initiate. Peter commands the church to receive these challenges this way:

1 Peter 5:5

All of you clothe yourselves with humility toward one another, because God resists the proud, but gives grace to the humble.

God's grace is mediated in the context of mutual humility in relationships. Without the humility to be challenged, we cannot grow. The requirement for a large amount of humility highlights why commitment to the church family is so important. It is very natural to isolate ourselves from direct challenge in our lives — it can be very uncomfortable when people call us out! However, God designed our discipleship journey to occur in the context of the church and in relationship with one another for the purpose of creating healthy opportunities for us to be challenged and called out.

Hebrews 13:17

Obey your leaders and submit to them, since they keep watch over your souls as those who will give an account.

In the West, where individual autonomy is the ideal, the concept of submission towards one another is profoundly counter-cultural. Jesus' command against "judging one another" (Matthew 7:1-3) is often quoted. Jesus' command, however, must not be interpreted as an invitation to total moral relativism or the freedom to self-determine what is right or true.

For example, in addressing a case of moral degradation in the Corinthian church, Paul clarifies that while he is not particularly concerned about the behaviour of those who are not followers of Jesus, he is deeply concerned that the church was becoming tolerant of things that were not of Jesus:

1 Corinthians 5:12

For what business is it of mine to judge outsiders? Don't you judge those who are inside?

As disciples, we must be willing to both receive and to give the high call to live a life like Jesus.

Respond

How teachable would you say you are? Do you tend to react defensively when someone corrects you? Do you take it personally and beat yourself up? Discuss with your discipler.

Have you treated some aspects of your life as if they are not part of discipleship? Which parts of your life would you say you are the most teachable? Least teachable?

If God's grace is given to those who are humble, have you humbled yourself? In which ways might pride be lurking in your heart? Ask your discipler for their input.

How can you call the people you are discipling to develop a teachable spirit? Are they already teachable, or is it something that they struggle with?

What is one area in each of the people you are discipling that you can have a crucial conversation with them about? Remember that crucial conversations are about moving someone closer to an effective multiplying relationship with Jesus.

Summary

Crucial conversations are an important part of discipleship to see us continue to grow in our relationship with Jesus. We need others to help us identify our blind spots. In summary:

- Crucial conversations are essential to see people growing in their faith; we must be able to spur each other towards Christlikeness.
- Crucial conversations are modelled after Jesus, full of grace and truth.
- Teachability and humility are necessary for healthy discipleship.
- Often when we are struggling to receive a crucial conversation, it is because of an issue of pride in our lives.
- Before we can effectively lead these discipleship conversations, we must be able to receive them ourselves.
- We always speak the truth in love so that people will be built up and encouraged.

Further Scripture Reading

If you would like to read more scripture on the topics in this session, please read:

- ☐ Matthew 23
- ☐ Matthew 4:17-19
- ☐ Matthew 7:1-3

Questions for My Discipler

Write down a few questions that you would like to talk about with your discipler.

Discipleship Session 19

☐ Prayer

Spend time together in prayer, invite the Holy Spirit to guide your conversation. Take a moment to sit in silence as you prepare to listen to God's leading.

☐ Celebration

What can you celebrate since you last met? How is God moving in your lives? What discipleship stories can you share?

☐ Review Previous Session

Take a moment to review the previous session. Are there any discussion points or items that you need to follow up on?

☐ Scripture

Read two passages of scripture from the ones used in the session. Choose one that encouraged and one that challenged you.

☐ God

What are the primary attributes that you learned about God's character in this section? What encouraged or challenged you?

☐ Yourself

What did you learn about yourself from the above passages?

☐ Obedience

Does what you learned change the way you think?

Does what you learned about change the way you act?

Does what you learned about change the way you treat others?

☐ Questions

Take a moment to talk through the questions you had.

☐ Next Step

What is one step you can take between now and your next session to practice what you learned?

Who can you share what you learned with to help them know Jesus?

☐ Pray

Share concerns. Pray for one another. Invite the Holy Spirit to help you.

☐ Next Discipleship Session _____

20
Leading Believers

Welcome to your 20th discipleship session. This is the second on crucial conversations, and it will focus on strategies for leading them. Take a moment to pray for the people whom God has entrusted you to disciple.

Scripture Reading

To help you prepare, read the following scriptures on your own:

- ☐ Hebrews 12:11-17
- ☐ Matthew 18:15-17
- ☐ 2 Timothy 3:16-17
- ☐ Ephesians 4:31

Respond

From the Matthew 18 passage above, how would you summarize Jesus' teaching on handling conflict?

What do these passages of Scripture reveal to you about the heart of crucial conversations or discipline? Why is this important?

Leading with Humility

Jesus' words about leading and speaking into each other's lives naturally leads us to the need for humility when speaking into someone's life. On the leading side of the conversation, we need the humility to listen to the person and take the time to earn their trust before we can speak. It is tempting to barge into a relationship without having taken the time to earn trust. However, humility and patience are vital in these conversations in order for us to speak from a place of credibility.

We must take the time to understand why those we are discipling are making decisions the way they are. If we are not careful, a crucial conversation can become simple instructions for people to do what we do — as if our approach is the only valid approach. The objective in discipleship is not to produce clones of ourselves but to see people made more like Jesus. When approaching a crucial conversation, we must take the time to evaluate the driving rationale behind the issue we wish to discuss. In many cases, there is more going on in that person's life than we realize. The basic building block of this requirement for humility is the process of asking probing questions about the person we are discipling. We must resist the urge to immediately share our perspective but first seek to understand the person and demonstrate that we are coming from a place of care and compassion.

Further, we cannot speak from a place of hypocrisy. Discipleship is about transformation, so we cannot disciple people towards a transformation that we ourselves are not open to. Discipleship is not a process where we merely dispense information. Rather, discipleship is a process where we invite people to examine our own lives and thereby see Christ at work. For this reason, we must have the humility to recognize that we ourselves are imperfect disciples.

Leading with Boldness

The second necessary component in a crucial conversation is the need for the boldness to confront the issue at hand. Often, our primary objective in a crucial conversation is to avoid hurting the other person's feelings. Many of us approach conversations with a general fear of conflict. However, hurt feelings or conflict themselves are not problematic; in fact, they can even be essential to growth. Jesus was bold with his words and certainly created conflict with them at times. Check out Matthew 23 to see how he addressed the leaders of the day. When we have taken the time to humbly listen and build trust over a long period of time, we can, and must, speak with clarity and boldness into the lives of the people we are discipling.

In our culture, we are often fearful of offending others. Such a fear can result in a timidity in our faith and will ultimately eliminate our discipleship effectiveness. We cannot see people move closer to Jesus if we are not willing to challenge them when they are moving in the wrong direction or not moving at all. The responsibility of the discipler in a disciple-making relationship is to engage in the difficult conversations needed to see someone develop gospel fluency, security identity, missional living, radical generosity and crucial conversations. All of the Discipleship Emphases are profoundly counter-cultural, and as a result, it is essential that we are continually pointing disciples back to the Kingdom principles they represent. It is not enough to merely address sin or moral failure; rather, we must boldly call people to adopt the revolutionary and missional ways of thinking and living that the scriptures call us to.

Practically speaking, we will require boldness to speak into the sensitive areas of a person's life such as finances, relationships, job, family, career and identity. While we need to first examine our own heart and motives and ensure that we are developing a clear theology and understanding of what we are boldly calling people to, if we are not willing to challenge someone in these areas, who will? Hebrews 12:11 clearly reminds us that sometimes the conversations, and discipline, will not be enjoyable, but in the long run, it produces tremendous fruit.

Hebrews 12:11

No discipline seems enjoyable at the time, but painful. Later on, however, it yields the peaceful fruit of righteousness to those who have been trained by it.

We may be afraid of consequences such as a tense relationship, losing a team member or failed discipleship. However, when we do not engage the tough conversation, we will eventually fail as a discipler no matter what. The types of issues that require boldness in our conversations will not address themselves on their own. As a result, eventually the issue will grow until it causes a major issue or crisis. The moment we fail to do what we know we need to do because we are afraid of the consequences, we are no longer actually leading or discipling that person — they can even be indirectly leading us. Summoning the humility and the boldness to address issues will, when done properly, often result in greater trust and a deeper relationship. Delaying the conversation will exacerbate the issue, and if left too long, may even make it nearly impossible to correct. It is for these reasons that crucial conversations are a critical discipleship emphasis. Without them, the entire discipleship process would break down.

Hebrews 12:15

Make sure that no one falls short of the grace of God and that no root of bitterness springs up, causing trouble and defiling many.

Unaddressed issues will have a communal effect on the multiplication effectiveness of the whole community. For example, unaddressed bitterness will have the effect of "defiling many" (Hebrews 12:17). Paul, in 1 Corinthians 5:13, instructs us to boldly address issues and, where there is unrepentance, to remove the capacity for evil to propagate. In case the necessity for boldness in our discipleship has not been convincingly addressed yet, Jesus provides us with a process in Matthew 18:15-17 to confront issues head on, whereby we graciously, but firmly, escalate a discipleship or relational issue.

It must be stated that the source of the boldness is not our own wisdom or experience alone. Rather, our boldness must be rooted and derived from a clear understanding of scripture. Scripture alone must be the primary source of our wisdom and experience, which, in turn, provides a foundation for our boldness. Only when we have been transformed by the truths revealed in the scriptures can we properly speak into someone's life.

2 Timothy 3:16-17

All Scripture is God-breathed and is useful for teaching, rebuking, correcting and training in righteousness, so that the servant of God may be thoroughly equipped for every good work.

Respond

Are there any areas of bitterness in your life or in the lives of those you are discipling that need to be addressed as soon as possible?

When you are seeking to have a discipleship conversation, how much do you rely on scripture as your source of wisdom? How can you develop this practice?

Have you taken sufficient time to earn the trust of the person you are discipling in order to speak to the issue? Does the person know that you care about them?

Do you avoid crucial conversations out of fear of how someone will respond? What could you do to address this?

Radical Candor

We have discussed the juxtaposing principles of invitation and challenge, grace and truth, and humility and boldness in laying the groundwork for crucial conversations. Kim Scott, a former

Google executive, developed a useful framework for helping managers in large organizations develop effectiveness in their leadership called *Radical Candor*. While this framework was not developed with the above discipleship context in mind, it is tremendously helpful for articulating the ideas. What follows is a brief summary and adaptation of the framework for a discipleship context. [26]

Radical Candor Grid

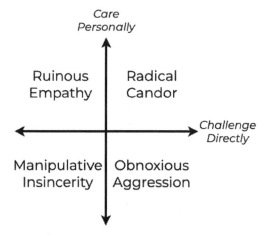

The two primary ingredients in an effective discipleship relationship are 'caring personally' and 'challenging directly.' Put simply, 'caring personally' is the genuine care shown for another person that, over time, allows trust to build. 'Challenging directly' is the willingness to confront the issues at hand when they present.

As shown above, when these two traits are functioning properly together, it is what Scott calls 'Radical Candor.' We sometimes call this 'family zone,' as it should be characteristic of a healthy church family and would be similar to the tone of relationships described above with "humility and boldness."

However, when either 'caring personally' or 'challenging directly' are not present, the results can be quite severe, even disastrous.

Firstly, where relationships are characterized by high care but low challenge, we find ourselves in 'Ruinous Empathy.' In this quadrant, we avoid crucial conversations out of a fear of how it will go. The results of avoiding the conversation are often ruinous for the person we are avoiding having the conversation with. We harm them by allowing them to continue in a pattern of unhealthy thinking or behaviours that they may be unaware of. It may feel empathetic to avoid addressing an issue, but it is ultimately unkind and unempathetic because we hurt that person in the long term. It is typically our own insecurity and fear that causes our inaction, not genuine compassion or empathy.

Conversely, when relationships are characterized by high challenge but low care, we find ourselves in 'Obnoxious Aggression.' 'Obnoxious Aggression' is what occurs when we challenge a person directly but do not have the credibility or trust to do so. It can also be obnoxious because of the tone or delivery of the feedback. The results of obnoxious aggression are relationships that are tense and fractured. However, we would advocate that in many cases, we must move from 'Ruinous Empathy' to 'Obnoxious Aggression' in order to find our way to 'Radical Candor.' We may overstep the bounds and enter 'Obnoxious Aggression' when trying to engage in a candid conversation. However, when we do so with humility and allow room for feedback, we can mature into 'Radical Candor.'

Lastly, where relationships are characterized by low challenge and low care, we find ourselves in 'Manipulative Insincerity.' These are relationships that are passive-aggressive, self-serving and ultimately headed for disaster. Discipleship relationships do not exist for our benefit. We are being discipled for Jesus' glory so that we can better develop effectiveness as a multiplying disciple for Jesus. When we are the one doing the discipling, it is not for our interests but with the intent of maximizing Kingdom impact. As a result, we cannot tolerate 'Manipulative Insincerity' of any kind, ever.

A particularly good example in scripture of 'Radical Candor' is found when the prophet Nathan confronts David for his sin with Bathsheba in 2 Samuel 12. He masterfully blends caring personally and challenging directly to see David repent from his sin and receive forgiveness.

Respond

Are you more prone to ruinous empathy or obnoxious aggression? What does your discipler think?

What kinds of issues do you find the most difficult to address? Why do you think that is? What about the easiest?

Is there a time that someone has been radically candid with you? What did they do well?

Summary

Crucial conversations with those we are discipling are particularly important to see our disciples grow.

- Fear of how people respond can paralyze us with fear; instead of staying in this fear, we boldly and graciously engage the issues for the health of those we are discipling or in relationship with.
- We must care personally and challenge directly.
- The source of our wisdom is scripture, not ourselves.
- Each person has a different bias for ruinous empathy or obnoxious aggression. Being aware of our biases can help us be more effective in our discipleship.

Further Scripture Reading

If you would like to read more scripture on the topics in this session, please read:

- ☐ 2 Samuel 12
- ☐ Matthew 16:13-28

Questions for My Discipler

Write down a few questions that you would like to talk about with your discipler.

Discipleship Session 20

☐ **Prayer**

Spend time together in prayer, invite the Holy Spirit to guide your conversation. Take a moment to sit in silence as you prepare to listen to God's leading.

☐ **Celebration**

What can you celebrate since you last met? How is God moving in your lives? What discipleship stories can you share?

☐ **Review Previous Session**

Take a moment to review the previous session. Are there any discussion points or items that you need to follow up on?

☐ **Scripture**

Read two passages of scripture from the ones used in the session. Choose one that encouraged and one that challenged you.

☐ **God**

What are the primary attributes that you learned about God's character in this section? What encouraged or challenged you?

☐ **Yourself**

What did you learn about yourself from the above passages?

☐ Obedience

Does what you learned change the way you think?

Does what you learned about change the way you act?

Does what you learned about change the way you treat others?

☐ Questions

Take a moment to talk through the questions you had.

☐ Next Step

What is one step you can take between now and your next session to practice what you learned?

Who can you share what you learned with to help them know Jesus?

☐ Pray

Share concerns. Pray for one another. Invite the Holy Spirit to help you.

☐ Next Discipleship Session _____

21
Leading Non-Believers #1

Welcome to your 21st discipleship session. This is the first of two sessions that will focus on crucial conversations with non-believers, also known as evangelism. Take a moment to pray for those that Jesus is asking you to introduce to him!

Scripture Reading

To help you prepare, read the following scriptures on your own:

- ☐ Revelation 12:11
- ☐ Acts 17:16-34
- ☐ Colossians 4:5
- ☐ Matthew 10:16

Respond

When you meet people who do not know Jesus, do you genuinely desire that they know Jesus themselves? How can you grow your passion for the lost?

Crucial Conversations with Non-Believers

The above discussion about crucial conversations with believers would also apply with non-believers. Of course, we must approach those relationships with equal humility and boldness. When considering a crucial conversation with a non-believer, we can break the process into four components: the messenger, the recipient, the message and the Spirit.

The Messenger

As we discussed in the section detailing gospel fluency, the Gospel is something that is known from both an intellectual and a relational standpoint. As a result, our discussion on communicating the Gospel must start with the messenger. Revelation 12:11 declares that it is our testimony that ultimately overcomes the enemy and will see people come to know Jesus.

Revelation 12:11

They conquered him by the blood of the Lamb and by the word of their testimony; for they did not love their lives to the point of death.

In other words, it is our lives and the story that Jesus is telling through them that leads to people knowing Jesus. Yet again, we can see the intersection of inner-life and outer-life aspects of discipleship. As our lives are transformed, the effectiveness of our testimony increases as well. As the Discipleship Emphases are formed in us, they will also be formed around us. A clear, bold and authentic testimony about what Jesus is doing in us will also see the world around us attracted to know Jesus. When we speak of the messenger, there are two components to highlight: integrity and authenticity.

Integrity

Oftentimes, those who do not know Jesus will highlight that the greatest critique they have of Christians is that of hypocrisy. This critique can cause us to be timid in our witness for fear that if we invite people to examine our lives, they will not like what they see. If there is a glaring issue in our lives that we are aware of and have not addressed, that is a major issue for which we should immediately repent and seek accountability. However, this does not mean that we should be slow or timid to share the Gospel but rather that we should be quick and eager to repent. We must continually submit ourselves to the way of Jesus and ensure that what we say we believe and what we actually do are in alignment. As followers of Jesus, our integrity is paramount. Our lives need to be blameless (Titus 1:6) and innocent (Matthew 10:16), and we must be wise in our relationships (Colossians 4:5).

It is worth mentioning that perfection is not the issue; rather, integrity is. Our aim is to ensure that the way we live and the way we talk about Jesus are congruent. When we pridefully present ourselves as being "perfect" or "having all the answers," we are setting ourselves up for failure because we are never perfect or all-knowing. This usually is expressed when we are more interested in being correct, winning debates and espousing our view, than we are in compassionately listening to and understanding the roadblocks to someone accepting Jesus. The goal is to help people see Jesus in us, not merely to communicate an idea. We point to ourselves, even in our weakness, so that people can see Jesus in us. When we acknowledge that we are imperfect but communicate our joy and satisfaction in Jesus and thankfulness for his grace in spite of our imperfections, our witness can be amazingly effective. The invitation to integrity and humility in our communication means that even a brand-new believer who still has many areas that need to be refined can be an effective evangelist. While they are not yet perfect, they can joyfully point to the work that Jesus has done in them.

Simply put, our witness is built on Jesus' grace, not our perfection. Our behaviour only becomes an issue when our words and actions are not in alignment. The invitation to know Jesus is an invitation for sinners to receive grace. Our message is not primarily about convincing someone of information so much as it is about inviting them to accept Jesus as King and join his Kingdom. That invitation will only make sense to the hearer when they can clearly see that Jesus is, in fact, our King.

Authenticity

Oftentimes, the greatest barrier to our ability to see people around us know Jesus is our fear. If Jesus is actively transforming and forming us, the work will be immediately and naturally apparent to all those who see it — if we will let them see it! Many of us produce an "edited" version of our lives. Jesus may be working in us, prayer may be a natural part of our rhythms and living with bold faith may be our norm. However, often when we talk to those who do not know Jesus, our love of him and his work in our lives is edited out and removed from the conversation.

When we authentically and genuinely talk about our faith in a natural way, it is a powerful witness. We naturally talk about the things we are passionate about, so why do we edit Jesus out? Oftentimes, it is from a fear that we will be ridiculed, that we don't know the answers or even that we have not developed a habit of talking about spiritual things. Each of those hesitations are indications of a need for deeper discipleship work in our life. However, those fears are best overcome by naturally beginning to flex our evangelistic muscles. When we naturally invite people into our lives and allow them to see and hear how Jesus is working, they will respond.

Respond

When you meet people who do not know Jesus, are you comfortable sharing about your personal relationship with Jesus in an honest and genuine way? Why or why not?

Have you taken the time to think through your personal testimony and relationship with Jesus so that you can share it with others?

Are there aspects of your life that you know do not exhibit a Christ-like character? Discuss these with your discipler and ask them to help you build a plan to live with greater integrity.

The Recipient

When we are engaging in conversations with non-believers, we must take the time to understand who we are talking to. When we are talking to someone about Jesus, there are both contextual and cultural issues as well as individual issues that we must take into account.

Context

When we are communicating the Gospel to someone, we must take the time to understand their context: specifically, their worldview and culture. The Gospel will always be understood by people through the lens of the cultural context in which they find themselves.[27] The context could include things such as race or ethnicity, religion or economic position. Communicating the Gospel to a Hindu will take a very different form than communicating the Gospel to a Muslim or an Atheist. Similarly, we must humble ourselves and take the time to understand how others understand the world. In the same way that the Apostle Paul took time to understand the Greeks in Acts 17 or adjusted his own lifestyle to suit those he was trying to reach in 1 Corinthians 9, we must be culturally flexible and wise. The objective is not to export our view on culture but to lead people to Jesus.

Individual History

In addition to the broad cultural issues briefly mentioned above, there are also individual considerations to take into account. As we will discuss later, discipleship involves inviting people into our world and opening our lives up to them. However, it is not just about us; we must take the time to understand the unique story of each person we are engaging with the Gospel. They may have specific and unique objectives or hesitations in hearing about Jesus. Perhaps a past hurt or fear due to family pressures. Regardless, we must compassionately and graciously take the time to understand who we are trying to reach. Communicating the Gospel is a three-way exchange between us, the Holy Spirit and the person we are trying to reach. Too often, we are too quick to give our perspective and not humble enough to understand the person we are talking to. A great tool is to ask probing and honest questions.

Respond

When you meet people who do not know Jesus, do you take the time to listen to them and get to know their personal and cultural heritage? Are you cultivating a genuine desire to learn more about other people?

Take some time to write out a few questions that you could ask people to get to know their unique story.

Have you taken the time to understand the basics of other faith systems? Which ones do you not know anything about?

Do you respect and value the perspective of others while compassionately calling them to surrender to Jesus? How might you simultaneously be more understanding while walking in greater confidence in knowing that they need to know Jesus?

Summary

Evangelism does not have to be complicated, intimidating or even awkward. Sharing our faith with non-believers is often as simple as being honest about our own walk with Jesus, while intentionally listening and asking questions to help them know him. In particular, we discussed the following points:

- Our personal testimony is one of the most powerful tools that we have.
- We must be honest and genuine when talking about our church involvement with non-believers; do not edit out our love of Jesus!
- We must be conscious of discrepancies between what we say and what we do; hypocrisy is tremendously damaging to evangelism.
- We must take the time to listen to know the cultural, ethnic and religious backgrounds of the people we are talking to.
- We must be conscious of our own cultural biases when communicating cross-culturally.
- We must invest time to know each person's journey in life so that we can properly contextualize the Gospel for them.

Further Scripture Reading

If you would like to read more scripture on the topics in this session, please read:

- ☐ Titus 1:6
- ☐ 1 Corinthians 9:19-23

Questions for My Discipler

Write down a few questions that you would like to talk about with your discipler.

Discipleship Session 21

☐ Prayer

Spend time together in prayer, invite the Holy Spirit to guide your conversation. Take a moment to sit in silence as you prepare to listen to God's leading.

☐ Celebration

What can you celebrate since you last met? How is God moving in your lives? What discipleship stories can you share?

☐ Review Previous Session

Take a moment to review the previous session. Are there any discussion points or items that you need to follow up on?

☐ Scripture

Read two passages of scripture from the ones used in the session. Choose one that encouraged and one that challenged you.

☐ God

What are the primary attributes that you learned about God's character in this section? What encouraged or challenged you?

☐ Yourself

What did you learn about yourself from the above passages?

☐ Obedience

Does what you learned change the way you think?

Does what you learned about change the way you act?

Does what you learned about change the way you treat others?

☐ Questions

Take a moment to talk through the questions you had.

☐ Next Step

What is one step you can take between now and your next session to practice what you learned?

Who can you share what you learned with to help them know Jesus?

☐ Pray

Share concerns. Pray for one another. Invite the Holy Spirit to help you.

☐ Next Discipleship Session _____

22

Leading Non-Believers #2

Welcome to your 22nd discipleship session. This is our final session, and we will be focusing on crucial conversations and will wrap up our discussion on evangelism. Take a moment to thank God for how he has uniquely positioned you for influence in his Kingdom.

Scripture Reading

To help you prepare, read the following scriptures on your own:

- [ ] 1 Peter 3:14-16
- [ ] Ephesians 6:12-20
- [ ] Ezekiel 36:27
- [ ] 1 Corinthians 1:18-20
- [ ] Luke 10:1-12

Respond

What is the greatest obstacle that you have in sharing your faith with others? Why do you think that is?

The Message

With all of the comments about ourselves and the recipient, we must look at the message itself in engaging crucial conversations. We will briefly address the subjects of grace and truth, simplicity and apologetics. 1 Peter 3:14-16 provides a helpful framework through which we can articulate the message.

1 Peter 3:14-16

But even if you should suffer for righteousness, you are blessed. Do not fear what they fear or be intimidated, but in your hearts regard Christ the Lord as holy, ready at any time to give a defence to anyone who asks you for a reason for the hope that is in you. Yet do this with gentleness and respect, keeping a clear conscience, so that when you are accused, those who disparage your good conduct in Christ will be put to shame.

Grace & Truth

As discussed under gospel fluency, when we are introducing someone to faith, it is important that we communicate with both grace and truth. On the one hand, we compassionately and graciously invite people to respond to the Gospel, and on the other, we must help them see the reality of their sin. We cannot compromise the message itself. We must graciously but firmly remain fixed on the moorings of our faith. It is not much help to communicate a Gospel to someone that is so watered down that it becomes basically useless. In our context, an authentic and honest communication of the truth of the Gospel is normally the most winsome. When we have taken the time to understand the context and the individual, we can boldly begin to lead them to Jesus in all of his glory. We must have the confidence to communicate our faith without the fear of rejection. Not everyone will respond positively to the message, but our job is not to win over everyone but to faithfully bring the message of Jesus.

One important consideration in communicating the Gospel is that we do not need to focus on specific moral issues initially. Said another way, until Jesus is Lord of someone's life, we cannot expect them to live as if he was. Of course, following the commands of Jesus is the most life-giving way of living, but expecting someone to obey Jesus when he is not Lord of their life is nonsensical. As Paul highlights in 1 Corinthians 5:12, our job is not to morally judge those outside the church but to lead them to the truth of the Gospel first. Moral issues are certainly important, both inside and outside the church, but in communicating the Gospel, it is important that we lead people to Jesus so that Jesus can do the work of sanctification in their lives when they receive him. Justification precedes sanctification every time. We are all sinners in need of a saviour, so focusing on a specific sin is beside the point when we are communicating the Gospel. This is something of a challenge because awareness of our sinfulness is important in leading someone to receive the grace of Jesus. This is why, as we will discuss below, the Holy Spirit is so important in the process. One helpful strategy is to ask genuine and empathetic questions about why someone is making the decisions they are so that we can understand how to best articulate the Gospel in a way that speaks to their specific story.

Simplicity

An important consideration when communicating the Gospel is that of simplicity. We can very quickly end up in all sorts of "theological weeds" and confuse both ourselves and them. The communication of the Gospel is not a primarily intellectual process, although our intellect must certainly be involved. If we are not careful, we can engage in fruitless discussion around interesting philosophical ideas without making any progress with the Gospel. When we are leading someone to Jesus, the objective is to look for those whose hearts are tender and receptive to the Gospel. That is not to say that we should not pray for and witness to those whose hearts are hard towards the Gospel. Rather, we should be aware of when someone is resistant to the message and distracting us with interesting conversations but has no real intention of engaging the message themselves.

Apologetics

Lastly, in communicating the message, we will need to have some awareness of apologetics. Apologetics is the discipline of well-reasoned arguments in defence of our faith. These could include scientific, historical, psychological or philosophical arguments. Many people will have legitimate questions about the veracity of the Gospel. It is important that we are familiar with the major arguments in defence of the faith in these major arenas. We do not need to know all of the answers, but we do need to know enough so that we can demonstrate that we have taken seriously the reliability of what we believe. If we have not even taken the time to ask if scripture is reliable, why should someone listen to us?

The specific apologetic strategies will be largely dependent on the people we are talking to. It is important to have taken time to understand the context we are speaking into. One interesting anecdotal observation from recent years is that the highly rational, scientific and philosophical apologetic arguments developed in the 20th century appear not to hold as much sway as they used to. In their place, psychological and personal arguments appear to be more impactful. The Gospel is not just truth in an abstract, depersonalized sense; it is also true because it helps us make sense of the world in a more individualistic sense.

It is important to remember that while apologetics can be a powerful evangelistic tool, very few people have ever been argued into a relationship with Jesus. The goal of apologetics is not to win arguments and prove to others that we are right. Instead, it is a tool to both show that we have taken our faith seriously and bring light into any legitimate questions that someone may have on their journey to a relationship with Christ.

The incredible news is that the Gospel can speak truth into any darkness. Our job is to understand how to do that into each context that we engage with.

Respond

Do you tend to communicate the Gospel in terms of moral issues or an invitation to a relationship with God?

Do you find yourself getting sucked into debates with people when you share the Gospel? How might you refocus the conversation on a relationship with Jesus?

Do you feel like you need all the answers when you share your faith? How might you adopt a more authentic and humble approach?

Check out the apologetics resources at engage.liftchurch.ca. Which area of apologetics are you the strongest in? Which one are you the weakest in?

The Spirit

The final, and perhaps most important, component of crucial conversations with non-believers is the role of the Holy Spirit: specifically, in empowering and preparing us to communicate the message, as well as softening the other person's heart to receive it.

Prayer

Prayer is the starting point for all of our interactions in our faith, but especially in communicating the Gospel. Ultimately, our battle is a spiritual one that is fought on a spiritual playing field.

Ephesians 6:12

For our struggle is not against flesh and blood, but against the rulers, against the authorities, against the cosmic powers of this darkness, against evil, spiritual forces in the heavens.

So how do we pray? We pray for ourselves that we would be bold, gracious and true. But we also pray that the message will be received and that hearts will be ready to receive it. In Exodus 7:3 and Ezekiel 36:27, God demonstrates that he can actually soften, or harden, hearts towards him so that his purposes can be fulfilled.

We must continually be in prayer to see the Holy Spirit prepare the hearts of those we are communicating to and equip us to articulate clearly his message of life. Inviting people to know Jesus can be both scary and vulnerable, so we must rely on the Holy Spirit to do the work — not just on our own strength. We must draw our boldness, courage and wisdom from him and trust that he is moving in others to prepare them to receive the message.

Ephesians 6:18-20

Pray at all times in the Spirit with every prayer and request, and stay alert with all perseverance and intercession for all the saints. Pray also for me, that the message may be given to me when I open my mouth to make known with boldness the mystery of the gospel. For this I am an ambassador in chains. Pray that I might be bold enough to speak about it as I should.

We cannot save anyone by ourselves, and we must ask the Holy Spirit to move so that his purposes can be fulfilled. The saving grace of Jesus is a miracle. That our hard hearts can be humbled such that we can understand and receive the Gospel is a miracle on par with the miracles of the New Testament. Apart from a move of God in us, we cannot possibly fathom his grace (1 Corinthians 1:18-20).

Power & Authority

When Jesus sends out the disciples in Luke 10, he gives them power and authority; likewise, our final point is that we too have been given that same power and authority. Throughout the book of Acts, supernatural work accompanied the disciples. We should both expect and ask for God to move supernaturally in our situations today.

Why is this under crucial conversations? Because based on the testimony of the New Testament, we should expect God to move supernaturally in the lives of non-believers so that they can see and respond to the power of God. Think about how different our conversations introducing people to Jesus proceed when they are accompanied by the demonstrable work of God in their lives. Our world is craving answers to the situations and challenges they find themselves in. What if we were to speak with power and authority, flowing from the Holy Spirit, into those situations, the same as Peter did in Acts 3:6: *"But Peter said, 'I don't have silver or gold, but what I do have, I give you: In the name of Jesus Christ of Nazareth, get up and walk!'"*

Respond

Are you regularly and consistently praying for those you are seeking to introduce to Jesus?

How does the reality that evangelism is a spiritual battle, not an intellectual or emotional one, change your approach to introducing people to Jesus?

Have you ever invited God to move supernaturally through you in your efforts to communicate Jesus to others? Why or why not?

Summary

Evangelism can feel complex and overwhelming, but by focusing on a simple message and trusting the power of the Holy Spirit, it can be much more natural. Some important keys to remember:

- Focus on a clear message: specifically, their relationship to Jesus. Moral issues are secondary.
- Be full of both truth and grace; be clear and convicted as well as compassionate and kind.

- Avoid getting sucked into the 'weeds.'
- Apologetics are important to engage the genuinely curious but can be a distraction if the person merely seeks to debate.
- Evangelism is ultimately a spiritual battle that must be fought with spiritual weapons of prayer and a supernatural move of God.
- We need to step into the authority that Jesus has given us.

Further Scripture Reading

If you would like to read more scripture on the topics in this session, please read:

- ☐ 1 Corinthians 1:18-20
- ☐ Acts 3:1-6
- ☐ Acts 7

Find helpful apologetics resources at engage.liftchurch.ca.

Questions for My Discipler

Write down a few questions that you would like to talk about with your discipler.

Discipleship Session 22

☐ **Prayer**

Spend time together in prayer, invite the Holy Spirit to guide your conversation. Take a moment to sit in silence as you prepare to listen to God's leading.

☐ **Celebration**

What can you celebrate since you last met? How is God moving in your lives? What discipleship stories can you share?

☐ **Review Previous Session**

Take a moment to review the previous session. Are there any discussion points or items that you need to follow up on?

☐ **Scripture**

Read two passages of scripture from the ones used in the session. Choose one that encouraged and one that challenged you.

☐ **God**

What are the primary attributes that you learned about God's character in this section? What encouraged or challenged you?

☐ **Yourself**

What did you learn about yourself from the above passages?

☐ Obedience

Does what you learned change the way you think?

Does what you learned about change the way you act?

Does what you learned about change the way you treat others?

☐ Questions

Take a moment to talk through the questions you had.

☐ Next Step

What is one step you can take between now and your next session to practice what you learned?

Who can you share what you learned with to help them know Jesus?

☐ Pray

Share concerns. Pray for one another. Invite the Holy Spirit to help you.

☐ Next Discipleship Session _____

Living Sent

Conclusion:
Go, Disciple

Congratulations, you have completed all the sessions! We pray that your love of Jesus, ability to hear his voice and confidence in leading others to do likewise has grown. However, this is not the end. The call to live as a disciple-making disciple is a life-long endeavour, and today is another step on that journey. As you serve Jesus as a disciple who makes disciples, you have been given the supreme gift of serving as a link in the age-old chain of faithful disciples. As you disciple those around you to know and love Jesus, you are connecting future generations to the one who made them. As you go, there are five exhortations and encouragements to leave you with.

First, discipleship is an invitation to a relationship with the loving creator of the universe, and that is always where our own discipleship flows from. It is easy to turn discipleship, church and/or serving others into tasks that we complete. That will lead to exhaustion, frustration and burnout. The life-long journey of discipleship is nurtured in our lives as we first seek Jesus and his Kingdom. Keep nurturing the spiritual habits of time in scripture, prayer, confession and repentance. Choose a posture of praise every day. In short, set your eyes on Jesus and never take them off of Him.

Hebrews 12:1-2

Therefore we also, since we are surrounded by so great a cloud of witnesses, let us lay aside every weight, and the sin which so easily ensnares us, and let us run with endurance the race that is set before us, looking unto Jesus, the author and finisher of our faith, who for the joy that was set before Him endured the cross, despising the shame, and has sat down at the right hand of the throne of God.

Second, ensure you are in relationships where you are being discipled. The completion of these discipleship sessions does not mean that Jesus has completed his work; he is just beginning! This means that you must commit to your church family and invite people into your life. As disciples, we must continually maintain a posture of humility, remembering that we have not arrived at the destination. Rather, we must always live as fellow disciples, committing to walk in unity with Jesus and allowing him to continually use our church family to refine us.

Philippians 3:12-13

Not that I have already reached the goal or am already perfect, but I make every effort to take hold of it because I also have been taken hold of by Christ Jesus.

Third, commit to a life of service. Choose to be a helper: a giver, not a taker. Discipleship, as we've discussed at length, is a life of service where we fully embrace our identity as servants of Christ and passionately live to serve others. When your natural instincts rebel against this basic principle of discipleship, turn your eyes to Jesus. Ask him for strength and reposition your heart so that you can live as he lived — giving his life as a ransom for us!

Matthew 20:26-28

On the contrary, whoever wants to become great among you must be your servant, and whoever wants to be first among you must be your slave; just as the Son of Man did not come to be served, but to serve, and to give his life as a ransom for many.

Fourth, value everyone. It is easy to isolate ourselves as we grow from new Christians into mature disciples. The temptation can creep in to only associate with other mature Christians and "like-minded individuals," as we will naturally have more in common with them. We must remember and remain committed to evangelism and discipleship of new believers. We must not think of ourselves as too important to serve new disciples. Commit now to a life where you are always discipling new believers.

Romans 12:3-5

I tell everyone among you not to think of himself more highly than he should think. Instead, think sensibly, as God has distributed a measure of faith to each one. Now as we have many parts in one body, and all the parts do not have the same function, in the same way we who are many are one body in Christ and individually members of one another.

Sixth, live sent. Remember the mission to which Jesus has called you. As you enter this world, you do so as an ambassador who has been sent, a servant of the Most High God. You go as a child of the King who loves you enough to die for you. You go as one fully alive in the Hope of Jesus. There is no greater way to spend our lives than to lay them down at his feet and say, "Lord I will go where you send me!"

Lastly, begin this journey again with someone else. Take all that you have learned and invite someone else into this journey. Take this book and invite someone else to journey through these sessions with you as your disciple!

2 Corinthians 5:20

Therefore, we are ambassadors for Christ, since God is making his appeal through us. We plead on Christ's behalf, "Be reconciled to God."

So, go, be a link in the chain. Live sent.

Matthew 28:19-20 [ESV]

Go therefore and make disciples of all nations, baptizing them in the name of the Father and of the Son and of the Holy Spirit, teaching them to observe all that I have commanded you. And behold, I am with you always, to the end of the age."

Appendix: The Story of Scripture

The Gospel, is of course a story, that can be summarized as follows.

In the beginning was God: We believe in God; who is love and is the creator and sustainer of all things. He exists in perfect harmony as three persons-in-one (we call it the Trinity). The Father, Son, and Holy Spirit: a perfect, loving, and glorious relationship. Distinct among his creation, God made…

You and I: We believe that we were created for relationship with God: to love and know him, each other, and ourselves. In our pursuit of this, we were meant to be creative and adventurous. However, we decided that we were better off, and we…

Rejected God – and became alone: We believe that we have rejected relationship with God, and as a result are separated from him. We have a broken relationship with each other and the world around us. This rejection of relationship with God is the root of what the Scriptures call sin, and within ourselves, there is no solution. Thankfully…

We were given a promise: We believe that God immediately began a process of redemption to restore relationship with mankind. This was documented in what Christians call the Old Testament which still speaks to us today. God's promise to restore relationship culminated in…

A solution – JESUS: We believe Jesus is the complete, perfect and the only answer. As God himself, Jesus lived roughly 2000 years ago revealing the character of God, dying so that we could be forgiven, and being resurrected to life forever conquering sin, death and the spiritual enemies of this world. Because of this…

We can respond: We believe that to live in relationship with God, we need to first acknowledge our living apart from God, and then put faith in Jesus. When we do so, we are forgiven of our sin, brought back into relationship with God, and are filled with the Holy Spirit. This is called the Gospel – the Good News. As a sign of our faith in Jesus we are baptized in water, publicly declaring that we now live for Jesus, helping others experience him, and collectively becoming…

The Church: We believe that Church exists so that others could know the hope of Jesus. To help make this happen, Jesus gave supernatural ability to the Church as we carry out his mission. We will continue this mission until…

He Returns: We believe that Jesus will return to bring final justice to creation. There will be a new heaven and earth where those that have put their faith in Jesus will enjoy him forever, and those that have not will be forever separated from him.

We believe the Bible teaches these things: We believe the Bible teaches these things. It is accurate and authoritative in our lives. We read it often to better know God and walk in relationship with him.

Endnotes

[1] Bonhoeffer, Dietrich. The Cost of Discipleship (SCM Classics) . Hymns Ancient and Modern Ltd. Kindle Edition.

[2] Keller, Tim. The Meaning of Marriage. Riverhead Books, 2011, p185

[3] Lewis, C.S. Mere Christianity. HarperOne, 1952, 2001, Chapter 4

[4] Wright, N.T. Paul, Fortress Press, 2009, p 35

[5] N.T. Wright, The Resurrection of the Son of God, 707. Cf. Russ Dudrey, "What the writers should have done better: A case for the resurrection of Jesus based on Ancient Criticism of the Resurrection Reports" Stone Campbell Journal 3 (2000) p55-78

[6] Luther, Martin. The Epistles of St. Peter and St. Jude Preached and Explained. Kindle Edition. p70,71-72

[7] Lewis p199

[8] Wright. Paul. p114

[9] Newbigin, Lesslie. The Gospel in a Pluralist Society. Eerdmans, 1989, p92

[10] Quoted in Fernando, Ajith. The Call to Joy and Pain (Kindle Locations 393-394). Crossway. Kindle Edition.

[11] Gaffin, Richard. Biblical Hermeneutics 5 Views ed. Porter and Stovell. IVP Academic, 2012. p99

[12] Lewis. p98

[13] Fernando, Ajith. The Call to Joy and Pain. Crossway, 2007, Kindle Edition. loc 387-388

[14] Soren Kierkegaard, Kill The Commentators, ericsenglish.com/kill-commentators-text/

[15] Barth, Karl. The Epistle to the Romans. Oxford University Press, 1968, p53

[16] Butterfield, Rosaria Champagne. The Gospel Comes with a House Key. Crossway, 2018 Kindle Edition.

[17] Grieg, Pete. The Vision and the Vow. Relevant Books, 2004, p129

[18] Guder, D. Missional Church. Eerdmans, 1998, p189

[19] Ignatius' *Letter to the Romans,* quoted in John R. Tyson, Invitation to Christian Spirituality, Oxford University Press 1999, p55

[20] Finney, Charles. Lectures on Revival. Bethany House, 1988, p22

[21] Grieg. p19

[22] Ibid.

[23] Ibid.

[24] Spurgeon, Charles, The Statute Of David For The Sharing Of The Spoil, No. 2208

[25] Note: this is not to say that we do not consider if there is Godly stewardship of the resources we give. We have a responsibility to give radically to those who will steward those resources well.

[26] Scott, Kim. Radical Candor. St. Martin's Press, 2017

[27] Newbigin, Lesslie. The Gospel in a Pluralist Society, p189

Manufactured by Amazon.ca
Bolton, ON